Praise for C*

"Upon meeting Koni Benson and reading her work, I can say that she has had a profound impact on my own scholarship as an historian of social movements—particularly in terms of thinking about collaboration between aggrieved and insurgent communities and the production of knowledge. This is a brilliant and riveting project, and unlike most graphic histories, *Crossroads* centers women and women's political activity. . . . This is original history about which much of the world has very little knowledge. And the story of South African women's struggles for housing and against forced removals is an international story of women's struggles for the commons."

—Robin D.G. Kelley, distinguished professor of history at University of
California, and author of *Freedom Dreams: The Black Radical Imagination*

"*Crossroads is*, quite simply, beautiful. It is intellectual and appealing and everything one could hope for from this kind of project. It is a meaningful engagement with a deeply troubling and enormously significant past. Not only does it weave text and images together to their best effect, but this is also one of the most insightful studies of urban history and social movements in any medium."

—Trevor Getz, professor of African history at San Francisco State University
and author of *Abina and the Important Men: A Graphic History*

"Through the narratives of women's struggles told in an honest and compelling way, *Crossroads* is an essential activist's handbook. It is a long-awaited and important compilation that is fundamental in understanding how women rose up against oppression and dispossession."

—Nomusa Makhubu, artist, art historian, and curator in the School of Fine
Arts at the University of Cape Town

"Koni Benson and her colleagues have produced an excellent and colourful history of the people of Crossroads. Based on original scholarly research, the comic books bring to life the tribulations and resistance of poor black people, especially women, in the face of constant state violence. Their determination to organise and to struggle for the right to a decent life in Cape Town, whose authorities were determined to exclude them from the city, hold crucial lessons for contemporary movements of the poor and marginalised. The *Crossroads* comic books are a fine example of popular history and should be compulsory reading in our schools and communities."

    —Noor Nieftagodien, director of the History Workshop at the University of the Witwatersrand and author of *The Soweto Uprising*

"Nuanced in its storytelling, *Crossroads* draws on the best that graphic traditions have to offer: iconic imagery, bold and effective compositional frames, thick colour patches that recall the vivid life that survived the bleak years of apartheid, and wonderful characters, who speak from but also beyond their specific historical and geographical locations. *Crossroads* is thus both African and not, speaking as all good books do, to a variety of human situations, across our planet. A book that crosses genres, it is at once memory, history and a feminist fable. Suitable for all that can read and hold ideas in their heads, and who love a good tale."

    —V. Geetha, feminist historian and editorial director, Tara Books, India

"I am aware of this work because of its international circulation and reputation for advancing quality scholarship in original forms and formats. I cannot speak too highly of this series, which dramatizes African women's collective resistance to political oppression in a historically grounded yet accessible medium—what we have come to call the graphic history."

    —Antoinette Burton, professor of history, University of Illinois, Urbana, and author of *The Trouble with Empire*

"A significant collection of striking visual histories about the women-led struggle for spatial justice in Crossroads. Its artistic approach makes it inspiring for future history writing and making."

    —Nashilongweshipwe Mushaandja, Namibian performance artist and scholar, editor of *Owela: The Future of Work*

"Throughout history and across the globe, one characteristic connects oppressed women: the indomitable spirit to fight back. With storytelling skill and gritty drawings the *Crossroads* compilation reminds us of the sheroes who built and defended their homes and communities against a range of dehumanising and oppressive forces. It serves as a vehicle, steeped in the historical, but simultaneously allowing us to see our current selves in the lessons it lays bare. This comic book is an important contribution and popular education tool to the organising and mobilising agenda for activists everywhere fighting for justice, dignity, and freedom."
—Shereen Essof, director of Just Associates Southern Africa, and author of *Shemurenga: The Zimbabwean Women's Movement 1995–2000*

"The apartheid-era struggles of black people for the right to live in Cape Town and to keep their families together were nowhere more bitterly and bravely fought than by the women of Crossroads. Their story is one of courage and suffering, and of solidarity and betrayal in the face of relentless state oppression and political conflict within their communities. This extended graphic narrative brings their voices to the fore, and depicts with vivid imagery and incisive analysis how struggles within one community enact the complexity of national political conflicts."
—Karen Press, poet and author of *Emergency Declarations* and cofounder of Buchu Books

"Based on interviews with activists, this graphic book vividly brings to life women's organized resistance in apartheid South Africa. More than this, *Crossroads* connects this powerful struggle history and politics with today's struggles for social, economic, racial and gender justice, and decent housing for all."
—Aziz Choudry, McGill University and University of Johannesburg, author of *NGOization: Complicity, Contradictions and Prospects*

"Blending together elements from genres of classics illustrated and manga comics *Crossroads* graphically shouts out to readers to remember and to recount. Stark images combine with detailed in-depth analysis to provide a shocking reminder of the violence and divisions propagated within communities through the structures of apartheid and how these have persisted into the post-apartheid present. Yet *Crossroads* is also a history of hope, resistance and the ability to forge alliances particularly amongst groups of women over a twenty-five-year period. *Crossroads*

bring these powerful stories in from the margins of history to the forefront of struggles in the past and the present."
—Leslie Witz, senior professor of history, University of the Western Cape,
coauthor of *Unsettled History: Making South African Public Pasts*

"The work is cutting edge in the way it accessibly grapples with the continuities and discontinuities, and with collective not just individual, questions of injustice shaped in forced removals . . . it stands out in the way it articulates a critical set of historical debates that are deeply relevant for the present, and the dynamics that shape the city after apartheid, its contradictions, persistent inequalities, and injustices. . . . Originality, intensive, creative, co-production work and commitment is embedded and embodied in this publication. Its impacts live on in its use in activist pedagogy and in collaborative knowledge projects with movements and publics beyond the university."
—Sophie Oldfield, professor of urban studies, University of Basel–University
of Cape Town, coeditor of *The Routledge Handbook on Cities of the Global
South*

"This beautiful graphic history tells an important story about women's resistance in South Africa. The women squatters struggled to maintain their community and their housing over many years and during immense political changes. Their efforts are a beacon, and telling the history as an illustrated narrative should make the lesson of their group efforts more widely known and appreciated."
—Kathleen Sheldon, Center for the Study of Women at UCLA and author of
African Women: Early History to the 21st Century

Crossroads
I Live Where I Like
A Graphic History

Koni Benson

Illustrated by André Trantraal
              Nathan Trantraal
              Ashley E. Marais

Foreword by Robin D.G. Kelley

KAIROS

Crossroads: I Live Where I Like: A Graphic History
Koni Benson, André Trantraal, and Nathan Trantraal © 2021
This edition © PM Press

ISBN (paperback): 9781629638355
ISBN (ebook): 9781629638515
LCCN: 2020934739

Cover design by John Yates/www.stealworks.com
Layout by Jonathan Rowland

10 9 8 7 6 5 4 3 2 1
Printed in the USA

Contents

Acknowledgments

Our first thanks go to the activists involved in the Crossroads Women's Committee in the 1970s and 1980s and the Women's Power Group of the 1990s for the brave interventions and lessons on collective mobilization that we need more than ever in the ongoing struggle to decolonize what has been deemed a "world-class city" (for some) in "the most unequal country in the world." Some of the over sixty life history interviews done with veteran activists involved in Crossroads have led to lifelong friendships and mentorships, and I am grateful for the ongoing conversation about the past and the present. Having begun this research fifteen years ago, many have passed on to join the ancestors and we are grateful for the actions, stories, memories, and reflections shared with a next generation. I also appreciate Mama Mene's consistent nudge to "make sense of this (current) nonsense" and to "make our history interesting to our children." A thesis gathering dust on a bookshelf does not indeed do justice to the history of Crossroads.

In particular, I would like to thank: Mama Jane Yanta, Mama Adelaide Mene, Nomangezi Muriel Mbobosi, Mama Eslina Mapisa, Mama Victoria Mkondweni, Mama Daisy Bara, Mama Viki, Mama Msaba, Mama Sigwela, Mama Tshingana, Mr. Lutango, Mama Selena Dasi, Mama Sylvia Ngozi, Mama Tomsana, Nomandla Tomsana, Mama Elsie Mkhumbuzi, Mama Weziwe Sogo-Hamse, Queen Hanoria Tynto Shugu, Mama Alice Mangqamba, Mama Nosipho Mgedzi, Mama Nomahobe Tom, Mrs. Dutoit Stuurman, Nontuthuzelo Jobela, Spokazi Luke, Gladys Nofemela, Mr. Oliver Memani, Mr. Sam Ndima, Mr. Mchobololo, Mr. Tomsana, Josette Cole, Michael Richman, Francis Wilson, Dot Clemenshaw, Selena Poswayo, Mama Poswayo, Siswe Yohane, Mama Winnie Nkosi, Nozuko Peters, Mrs. Ndyalvane, Mrs. Millicent Nongxa (Ngxobongwana), Mama Adelaide Ngqokomashe, Mrs. "Ten Ten" Mwezo-Ndzunge, Zodwa Tika, Mama Tandeka Tika, Mr. Melani,

Mr. Zingisile Mnyukweni, Mr. Ndyalvane, Mr. Mandla Sihlali, Mama Nozamile Beme, Mama Conelia Kwinana, Agrinette Kwana, Mama Kontyolo, Mama Nophelo Xhapha, Mama Nolula Mzikulu, Mama Thobeka Ngxiya, Mama Ntombentsha Mdyeshana, Mama Mwanda-Tika, Nondumiso Nosisi Mbeka, Mama Eunice Totose, Mama Nomvuyo Alice Nqimtza, Aunt Susan Conjwa, Mama Mangqamba, Mama Mgedzi, Mama Tom, Mama Jobela, Mlungisi Noludwe, Mr. Ntwasa, Mr. Mfana, Anne Greenwell, and Malibongwe Sopangisa.

A special amandla-filled thank you to all of the participants in the People's History Courses at the International Labour Research and Information Group's (ILRIG) Globalization Schools where we studied the history of society we face and plotted ways forward for the society we need. It was those conversations, discussions, and debates in ILRIG workshops, between 2006 and 2014, which determined the most important themes from the history of Crossroads to draw out in this book. From the Community Activist Course, I would like to especially thank: Khusta, Faeza, Ebrahiem, Eve, Mary Tal, Lorraine, Eleanore, Lucille, Joyce, Biko, Mhlobo, Farieda, Levona, Valecia, Winifred, Waagiedah, Layla, Johanna, Valerie, Pupa, Zikona, Soga, Nokuzola, Nwabisa, Mthobeli, Shereen, Matilda, Roegshanda, Mashane, Antonio, Mastoera, Ashley, Ricardo, Charney, Deborah, Willy, and Viwe. From all of the BWA and BWL workshops and conversations on gender dynamics of, and organizing against, racism, sexism, and neoliberalism in those years, I thank: Wendy, Sarah, Yolanda, Jean, Sarah, Selina, Dora, Kim, Rachmat, Noncedo, Valerie, Mary, Nopasika, Fowzia, Maureen, Valarie, Nomaxabiso, Myrtle, Sive, Bridgette, Alfreda, Noxolo, Andiswa, Sarah, Viwe, Zikhona, Nicholene, Noma, Judy, Shereen, and Anna.

When I first showed the comic books to Mama Yanta, she flipped through the pages, pausing to say, I remember that day . . . and that day . . . and, wow, *that* day. This is thanks to the talented hands and sharp eyes of André, Nathan, and Ashley who worked their magic to weave ideas, words, and archival photos, into illustrations that bring people, issues, debates, dynamics, lines, landscapes, tones, realities, and the moods of the layers of this story together. When we first started this project in 2012, we thought we would do one twelve-page comic book. Eight years later and 161 pages later, I have learned so much from this collaboration and am grateful for the art/work, the humour, the ethics, and the friendships this journey has brought into the world at large and into my little life in particular.

This book grew out of a six-part comic book series that would not have been possible without the interest, encouragement, and support of: Isotrope Media, in particular Stefan Blank, for printing and launching the first book of the series in 2012. Thank you to my coworkers and comrades at ILRIG, Ronald, Anna, Mthetho, Judy, Michael, Shawn, Anele, Mzi, Nandi, Nomonde, Phumeza, and Jeff. In particular I want to thank Leonard Gentle, for the space to run far and wide with creative popular political education initiatives, and for the encouragement to take study leave to write up the thesis in 2008 and then again to write the graphic novel series in 2014. Thank you to the African Centre for Cities Postdoctoral Fellowship Grant that made the writing possible, I am grateful for the space and support from Sophie Oldfield, Edgar Pieterse, and Henrik Ernstson.

The illustrations and printing of books 2 to 6 of the original series would not have been possible without the enthusiasm and the resources from: the Steelworkers Humanity Fund, in particular Doug Olthuis for book 1; Pro Helvetia, the Swiss Arts Council and the Swiss Agency for Development and Cooperation, for book 2; the Ontario Public Service Employees Union (OPSEU/SEFPO), in particular campaigns officer Luisa Quarta, for book 4 and 5; the Blue Planet Project at the Council of Canadians, in particular Meera Karunananthan for book 5; and the Department of Historical Studies at the University of Cape Town, in particular Lance van Sittert, for books 3–6.

Thank you for the engagement and feedback from students in the first run of my course "African History Through Comic Books: History for What and for Whom?," especially Zaynab, Malik, Monde, Aysha, Tannagh, Ally, Naledi, and Andrew, and for the same from Trevor Getz, Antoinette Burton, and Aziz Choudry. Many thanks to Allen Isaacman for the support throughout the original thesis research. I am grateful for the shared commitments to engaged teaching and the space to finish this book and to grow with my coworkers in the Department of History at UWC: Uma Dhuphelia-Mesthrie, Nicky Rousseau, Ciraj Rassool, Leslie Witz, Paolo Israel, Phindi Mnyaka, Bianca Van Laun, Andrew Bank, Riedwaan Moosage, Patricia Hayes, Janine Brandt, and Jane Smidt. Thank you to Nsika Kuhlane and Siyabulela Lengisi for bringing the thesis to life and into conversation with the District Six museum and the Crossroads Library, and for engaging this work in your search for creative ways to pass on this history to youth in Crossroads today.

This project has also benefited from feedback during and especially after presentations of the work, including at: the Berkshire Women's History

Conference in Canada in 2014; the Madras Institute of Development Studies in India in 2015; the UHURU Center at the University Currently Known as Rhodes, in Makhanda in 2015; the South African Young Academy of Science Symposium on Science and Society in Africa: Fact, Fiction, and Media: Re-Imagining Science Engagement and its Impact, Cape Town in 2015; the Radical(izing) Collaborations Through Academic Research: Possibilities and Limits, at the University of Cape Town in 2016; the CODESRIA Gender Symposium in Egypt in 2016; Greatmore Studios Great Talks Series on Popular and Elite Art Writing in South Africa: Frictions, Fictions and Functions, Cape Town in 2017; at Decolonizing Arts Education Forum in Namibia in 2017; Lephephe Print Gatherings at Keleketla Library in Johannesburg in 2018; the Caribbean Studies Association Conference on Education, Culture and Emancipatory Thought, in Cuba in 2018; and at the Zeitz Museum of Contemporary African Art in 2019 where Mama Mene dropped bars and bars and bars.

A huge thank you to all of the reviewers and to the good people of PM Press. We could not have found a better home for a book where there is no need to choose between commitments to historical scholarship, political activism, or graphic arts. Many thanks to Robin Kelley for the conversations, the care, the trails blazed for historians of social movements intervening in the politics of movement building now, and for the foreword to this book. I have read so many life-charting texts in conversation with the seeds you sew in your forewords, from Angela Davis's *The Meaning of Freedom* and Grace Lee Boggs's *Living for Change*, to C.L.R. James's *A History of Pan-African Revolt*. It is an absolute honour.

Last but, if anything, the opposite of least, we are grateful for the support of those we live and love with. From Nathan: Thanks to my mother, who raised her children alone. And to my wife and daughter who are constantly changing me for the better, be it the clothes I wear or the way I treat people. From André: Thank you to all the women who made tea so I could draw. Love you Charmaine Africa and Baby Spaghetti. From Ashely: To all those who have impacted my life in a positive way I am forever grateful: my mother the pillar of my life, and friends, and family. From Koni: in addition to all of the above, I give thanks for all the encouragement and inspiration from comic book heads, artists, history nerds, feminists, and Pan-Africanist activists friends, and family who took special interest in this project over the years and years, including: Ahmer, Jesse, Gwen, Laila, Terna, Indu, Sankara, Rucera, Awra, Richa, Ronald, Thuli, Ponni, Asher, Nix, Kelly, Leigh-Ann, Geetha, Terry, Anna, Elsbeth, Mushaandja, Dad, and Mom.

Foreword

ROBIN D.G. KELLEY

In order to convince my teenage son to accompany me to South Africa in the summer of 2016, I agreed to take him to a game reserve on "safari." I dragged him everywhere on an impromptu political tour—Soweto, the Hector Pieterson Museum, Robben Island, the Apartheid Museum, the Steve Biko Centre in Kingwilliamstown, Cape Town's District 6, the arts festival in Grahamstown/Makhanda, and every landmark and gravesite imaginable. And then we spent two days and nights at the luxurious Shamwari Game Reserve in the Eastern Cape. I chose it because it purported to be environmentally conscious and prohibited hunting. This was supposed to be a non-political part of our visit, a much-anticipated break from the cram course he was getting in the history of South African struggle.

As soon as we arrived, the staff assigned us to a beautiful lodge named after Sarili kaHintsa, the nineteenth-century Xhosa paramount chief who followed the prophesy of a fifteen-year-old girl named Nongqawuse, who in 1856 called on the people to kill the cattle and destroy the crops in order to incite the spirits to drive the white people out. The whites did not leave, but this didn't stop Sarili from attempting to build a united front of neighboring chiefs to drive out the British militarily. As it turned out, the lodge was named Sarili for a reason. We were on land he had once ruled, a fact we learned from the head of staff who had been working for Shamwari for over nineteen years. As we talked more and I disclosed more of my own politics and discomfort with being there, he matter-of-factly mentioned that his family had once owned land on what was now the reserve, was forced off the land and reduced to farm laborers, and subsequently were buried on this very land. Indeed, he was a direct descendant of Sarili himself! From that point on, every African we met employed by Shamwari spoke about the land and the dream of restoration, not as privatized wealth but as a source of livelihood, sustenance, reconstruction, nation-building. We couldn't help but notice the dilapidated shacks on the other side of the N2 highway where some of the employees of the big game reserves lived.

This was not supposed to be the "political" part of our tour, yet it was the most political, most illuminating experience we had had in South Africa. We listened to the workers share stories of resilience and resistance, dignity, and power, as well as dispossession, violence, and struggle for the commons. Taken together, their stories exposed how the language of creating commons for wildlife, preservation, conservation has been appropriated by the World Bank and private corporations in the service of privatization, turning capitalists into the environmental guardian of the planet, and in the name of protecting biodiversity and promoting eco-tourism have expelled indigenous people. The coup de grace was when the head of staff casually mentioned before rushing off to attend to guests that the property had just been sold to Dubai World.

This was people's history at its finest—vivid and truthful storytelling more powerful than anything I could have read in a scholarly book or seen in a museum exhibit. Reading this spectacular graphic series—*Crossroads: I Live Where I Like* by Koni Benson, illustrated by André Trantraal, Nathan Trantraal, and Ashley Marais—is the closest I've ever come to experiencing anything like our two days in Shamwari. It too is about land, livelihood, dignity, power, the commons, and resistance. And it is about women. Tracing a forty-year history of women-led struggles in a section of Cape Town targeted for demolition, *Crossroads* narrates the successful campaign to save this community of shack dwellers from imminent destruction and population transfer. Based on Benson's original archival research and oral histories for her doctoral dissertation, the stories here haven't been told before in any comprehensive or scholarly way, though the organizers did write and produce a play about the movement during the first wave of squatters' struggle during the late 1970s and early 1980s. Moreover, the series—chapter 1, in particular—sets up the confrontation between the shack dwellers and the state by tracing the long history of colonial settlement, dispossession, war, urbanization, and the state's efforts to formalize and codify apartheid. Resistance does not begin in 1975, in other words. In fact, the series reveals how these forms of resistance draw on established traditions of social and cultural life, as well as ruptures in class and gender relations generated by developments in South Africa's racialized political economy. And unlike most graphic histories, *Crossroads* centers women and women's political activity.

Yet this is not a story of unmitigated triumph. Their objective isn't simply to inspire new generations or uncritically reproduce iconic movement stories for the purpose of creating a monument to anti-apartheid struggles frozen in time and place. By illuminating the long history of settler colonialism in the Cape, these stories reveal the continuation of dispossession and enclosure (privatization of land and resources) in post-apartheid South Africa. The series captures the ebb and flow of people's power and shifts in governmentality in order to manage resistance while maintaining the post-apartheid state's legitimacy. In chapter 6, for example, Benson takes on the common narrative that the sit-ins organized by the Women's Power Group—three hundred women demanding state provisions of services and housing—were merely responses to the ANC's incompetence or capitulation to neoliberalism. Instead, she highlights how those struggles are linked to the longer history documented throughout the entire series and to the failure to fully dismantle the apartheid state following the formal extension of political rights.

Crossroads is also feminist history. It breaks new ground in its attention to gender and gender dynamics of collective organizing. Local leaders did not follow the traditional pattern of charismatic, masculinist leadership. On the contrary, the entire series provides a subtle critique of the assumption that charisma is a characteristic of leadership in insurgent social movements. And by looking at four decades of struggle, it quickly becomes clear that women were always at the forefront of struggles against displacement, slum clearance, poverty, and any attack on the commons.

Crossroads represents the very best in a tradition of radical graphic histories going back to Art Spiegelman's *Maus* series, through Marjane Satrapi's *Persepolis* and *Persepolis 2*, and Joe Sacco's outstanding *Footnotes in Gaza*. But these precursors generally take the form of memoir, despite their sustained attention to oral and archival sources, and they tend to focus on moments or encounters as mnemonic devices to tell longer histories. *Crossroads* is more ambitious in both form and content. In many ways, it is an outgrowth of "people's history"—the political and historiographical project that emerged in the 1970s with the publication of *History Workshop Journal* and the *Radical History Review*. South African social historians figured significantly in this trend, many having committed to writing "people's histories" of South African labor (mostly miners and agricultural labor) but doing very little to follow through on the promise of collaboration with those movements. *Crossroads* fulfills the promise of developing and implementing methodologies of collaboration, where historical actors and historians work in collaboration and dialogue—workshopping drafts of the comics with activists, generating a dialectic between archive and memory, producing new knowledge which then encounters and stimulates memory, dialogue, and a dynamic synthesis. This is not how history, at least academic history, is usually written. And it is dangerous work, especially given the current antagonisms between the state and shack dwellers in the Western Cape and throughout the country.

In short, it is impossible to read this book and not be moved in the way my son and I were moved listening to descendants of South African freedom fights speak about their ancestors and the future they hope to build for their progeny. What you have here is a riveting, original history about which much of the world has very little knowledge. And the story of South African women's struggles for housing and against forced removals is an *international* story of women's struggles for the commons. Women have been on the front lines of modern enclosure and have waged militant campaigns against commercial logging, land grabs, pesticides, and the like. They have adopted subsistence agriculture to defend their communities from the impact of structural adjustment and dependence on global markets. The destruction of subsistence economies in the rural areas has forced women into cities in the first place, and by extension into debt low-wage labor, domestic service, childcare, sex work—in other words, waged reproductive labor—all around the world. What *Crossroads* demonstrates is what happens when poor women collectively resist the limited options available to them and fight to hold the land. The fight also changes their relationship to one another, to the state, and to the land. And it will change you.

Introduction

Women in Crossroads were famous for their collective stance against apartheid bulldozers which forcibly "removed" and relocated 3.8 million black people from their homes and neighbourhoods between the 1960s and 1980s in the process of enforcing segregation and appropriating land for white people. In Cape Town, Crossroads was the only African informal settlement to *successfully* resist demolition, thanks to the organized resistance spearheaded by the Crossroads Women's Committee.

This book draws together a three-way conversation between art, activism, and African history. It builds on my PhD thesis research about histories of past and ongoing organized resistance to forced removals and collective struggles for access to what should be public services like housing, water, education, safety and so on taken up by two groups of women in Crossroads, Cape Town. Given the visible lack of change in the city in the decades after apartheid officially ended, I wanted to know what happened to the women involved in the Crossroads victory, as *community* activists who had not been part of political party leadership, underground movements, or women's movement structures that dominate narratives of anti-apartheid struggle history. I wanted to know what happened to them, the issues they stood for, and their histories.

I interviewed over sixty people who had been involved, studied state, corporate, and activist archival materials (reports, commissions, surveys, maps, affidavits, legal cases, interviews, newspapers, video footage, slides, photographs, posters), and drew on hundreds of books and articles. The thesis was titled "Crossroads Continues" because despite the lip service given to the important role of women in Crossroads and their role in bringing down apartheid segregation, and despite the grand narratives of 1994 being a triumphant turning point in the fight against apartheid, decades into what we can call the post-apartheid apartheid period, there has been minimal redistribution of resources.[1] Yet ongoing protest has been framed as everything from nostalgic, naive, impatient, and unrealistic to lawbreaking, queue jumping, and criminal. This criminalization of the dispossessed demanding justice is neither colour-blind nor unique to South Africa. There is a history, a racialization, and a gender dynamic to the ongoing brutality of the violence of neocolonial dynamics.

Crossroads: I Live Where I Like gets its name from the place that became Crossroads, and the ever-present crossroads we continue to navigate as we gather together to build a future that women in Crossroads fought for. *I Live Where I Like* is an echo of Black Consciousness leader Steve Biko in his column *I Write What I Like*, published between 1969 and 1972 in the South African Students' Organization journal (under the pseudonym "Frank Talk"), before his death in detention in 1977. Women in Crossroads likewise took matters into their own hands and insisted on being heard. They wrote or made history, collectively, in action, by movement, by a refusal to move, by a *we*, a We Shall Not Be Moved. *I Live Where I Like* is a collective social biography of two women-only movements in Crossroads in the 1970s and 1990s, brought into conversation with activist organizations in the 2000s working to politicize the need for public and political solutions to what racial capitalism frames as personal problems, including but not limited to housing.

In Cape Town over 460,000 families wait on official lists for subsidized housing, in a City that builds between eleven thousand and sixteen thousand low-cost housing units a year. Rather than die waiting for shelter, many people take matters into their own hands and get involved in action, in *activ*ism, in lobbying, in mobilizing, in protest, in refusing homelessness. In the midst of writing this book it was reported that there had been nearly three thousand protest actions in a ninety-day period, involving more than a million people.[2] The most common reasons given for these protests were grievances around land and housing.[3] More and more, rejecting what has become known as the

---

1 Koni Benson, "Crossroads Continues: Histories of Women Mobilizing against Forced Removals and for Housing in Cape Town South Africa, 1975–2005," PhD dissertation, University of Minnesota, 2009.

2 Max Du Preez, "Our Protest Culture Is Far from Dead," *Pretoria News*, February 11, 2014; Martin Plaut, "Behind the Marikana Massacre," *New Statesmen* August 20, 2012; Penwell Dlamini, "Gauteng under shack attack," *Times*, April 2, 2014.

3 Peter Alexander, "Rebellion of the Poor"; Nashira Davids, "Service-Delivery Protests Getting Uglier: report," *Times*, October 11, 2012; Carin Runciman,

myth of the housing waiting list,[4] residents are taking land, setting up shelter and food gardens on open fields, and facing brutal repression by the state in protection of private property. Calling in the police, the military, and private security forces to quell protest over access to basic services such as housing, water, health, and education is not unique to South Africa.

This book is the outcome of working with community-based activists in unpacking and challenging the racist and sexist history of Cape Town responsible for creating the current norms and binaries of capitalism that has created, and continues to reproduce, the current housing crisis. During and after my thesis work, I was working at the International Labour Research and Information Group (ILRIG) with housing activists and community organizers mobilizing around current evictions, homelessness, water cut offs, xenophobia, sexism, and inhumane working conditions. The history of Crossroads became an important tool for mapping out power dynamics and collectively studying the social construction of Cape Town that we face today. This was done in workshops and courses including: the 2011 and 2012 People's History Course; and the 2012–2013 Community Activist Course with participants from the Progressive Youth Movement, Informal Settlements in Struggle, Zille-Raine Heights, Hangberg, Tafelsig Community Forum, Women for Development, Abahlali baseMjondolo, Communities for Environmental Justice, the Anti-Eviction Campaign, Blikkiesdorp 4 Housing, United People for Homeless South Africans, Overcome Heights Informal Settlement Network, Vukuzenzele Housing Project, Gugulethu Backyarders, Gimpie Street, and the Delft Integrated Network. It also included discussion in the 2006–2011 monthly women-only public forum with activists from housing, food, water, farmworker, domestic worker, sex worker, migrant labour and refugee women's organizations, and in a 2008–2009 women's leadership course.

Unpacking the historical and gendered dynamics of land dispossession, shack dwelling, and organized struggles for housing was extremely important for thinking through how this city has been constructed, and how it can be

---

"An Overview of Community Struggles in 2012." Also see data provided by the Multi-Level Governance Initiative at University of the Western Cape.

4   Kate Tissington, Naadira Munshi, Gladys Mirugi-Mukundi, and Ebenezer Durojaye. *"Jumping the Queue," Waiting Lists and Other Myths: Perceptions and Practice around Housing Demand and Allocation in South Africa.* Community Law Centre, University of the Western Cape/Socio-economic Rights Institute of South Africa, 2013.

deconstructed and reconstructed. The histories of mobilization and demo-bilization of movements became powerful tools for exploring strategies in the struggle for the commons *and* for looking at the layers involved in how struggles and movements can be undermined even as they are being praised. How has the story of racism, sexism, and segregation in Cape Town been told? How have narratives been sanitized, appropriated, and used to dismiss, overlook, or justify growing inequalities? Who makes history? Who writes history? And how can histories about challenging authority, not reproduce that authority in the conventional hierarchical assembly line of producing history books? These are some of the guiding questions that impacted the ex-periments that became this book. More detailed discussions on interrogating the relationships between archives, authority, and accountability and between positionality, power, politics, and pedagogy, are available in a range of articles noted in the bibliography.

While engaging the history of Crossroads in these political education sessions, I drew on old film footage, shared interview transcripts, and used newspapers, and photographic archival material to put together a three-hundred-year timeline of a history of organized resistance to land dispossession in Cape Town. Piecing together and sharing such urgent and unfinished struggles from the past (i.e., the thesis research and education work) felt important, but I had (little time and) serious questions about the ethics of authorship and authority and doubted very many people would want to read a five-hundred-page thesis. The Aunties in Crossroads kept saying, "Make this as interesting to our children as it is to you. They think our stories are boring."

I was gifted the Trantraal Brothers comic book *Coloureds* for my birthday in August 2010. I had indeed been daydreaming about a *Boondocks*-meets-*Latino USA* version of (or even instead of) my PhD thesis, a way to draw out and share the most urgent slices of an unfinished history of organized resis-tance to segregation, homelessness, racism, and sexism in South Africa as a whole, but in the city of Cape Town in particular. I was surprised that taking a chance and calling the contact number on the back of the comic book during a break at work one day actually got me through to André Trantraal. And off I went to meet him and his brother Nathan. We spent hours talking and then months swapping comic books and graphic novels—*Palestine, Persepolis, Louis Riel, Abina*—variously named graphic narratives of nonfiction. Over time, they asked me to do some writing for a magazine project proposal they were involved with, and I asked them about the prospects of illustrating the Crossroads history. We had many conversations about our very different relationships to the history of Cape Town, approaches to politics, and thoughts on history and fiction writing.[5] We drafted a proposal that was variously rejected as too serious for comics and too playful for history.

In 2011 I was running a People's History Course at the ILRIG Globalisation School and the leader of a delegation of workers, attending through a partnership with the Steelworkers Humanity Fund, asked if the histories I had been sharing with the group were available to be shared with workers in Canada, Mozambique, and Brazil. "Well, funny you should ask . . ." and I told them about our vision. Much to my chagrin they invited us to put together a proposal in 2012, which resulted in our first funding in 2013. Halfway through book 1, Ashely joined the drawing team. In 2014, what became chapter 1 of the book you are about to read, was published by Isotrope Media, an independent Cape Town based publisher that publishes the work of emerging and established comic book artists/authors. I then took up a postdoctoral fellowship in order to have time to continue with this writing. Over the next two years we published the subsequent chapters, comic book by comic book, welcoming interest, solidarity, and support though the activist organizations and historical and urban studies research and teaching spaces I was involved with over time. This was part of both pushing for and welcoming the interest in critical approaches to people's history projects,[6] alternative modes of engaged scholarship, and creative approaches to researching and teaching history.[7]

---

5   For more details about some of the processes behind our collaboration, see Koni Benson, "Graphic Novel Histories: Women's Organized Resistance to Slum Clearance in Crossroads South Africa, 1975–2015," in "40th Anniversary of the Writing of African Women's History Part II," eds. Kathleen Sheldon and Judith van Allen, special issue, *African Studies Review* 59, no. 1 (2016): 199–214.

6   Prospects for these kinds of interventions by historians, committed to past and present cultures of resistance are elaborated upon in Koni Benson, "Drawing (on) the Past in Histories of the Present: Dialogues and Drawings of South African Women's Organized Resistance to Forced Removals," in Lifongo Vetinde and Jean Blaise Samou, eds., *African Cultural Production and the Rhetoric of Humanism* (Lanham, MD: Lexington Books, 2019), 127–49.

7   For more on how the series was used in teaching history, see Koni Benson, "A Conversation I Was Missing: Illustrating Learning Curves That Refuse a Straight Line, Zaynab Asmal Interviewed by Koni Benson," *Agitate Journal:*

But is it fact or fiction? Our approach to condensing five hundred pages of history into graphic art was to establish a chronological background of the context over time and to foreground the most important moments raised by the Crossroads Women's Committee and the Women's Power Group which resonated with frontline activists taking forward these movements today. It has been a creative endeavour to re-present and represent many knots and disparate threads. The multiple raids and demolitions over time have meant that most people who lived through this period of the history of Crossroads do not have many photographs or personal documents from the apartheid period. Working from old and new oral history transcripts, descriptions, memories, court testimonies, news footage, and other archival images, it has been possible to re-member these stories and re-create them into what is seen by those who were involved as a retrospective photo album, but which will inevitably take on different meanings to different readers and readings of the book. None of the characters or days depicted are made up. But they are of course selective and selected from particular positions and perspectives. The book draws on, and in the making created, sets of archives, which historian Michel-Rolph Trouillot points out are indeed motivated information.[8] After all, as historian Howard Zinn argues, you cannot be neutral on a moving train.[9] But after much debate about footnotes and longer text, we have tried to make obvious whose perspective is being given, where it came from, and where it can be found. The thesis is also available with formal and detailed referencing techniques, which are discussed in the Re:Sources section at the end.

It was not only because we received piecemeal funding that we did not initially publish a book—it was a conscious decision to produce a vibrant, grabbable, familiar comic book—using the same style of the Trantraal Brother's *Coloureds* to signify a rejection of the ways in which Cape Town's history has been as segregated as it's neighbourhoods (into the bounded apartheid categories of either White, Indian, Coloured, or Black). We had questions about our own authorship and were suspicious of precious,

---

Unsettling Knowledges vol. 2, March 2020, https://agitatejournal.org/article/rmfpreconceptions-of-a-movement-interview-with-zaynab-asmal/.

8   Michel-Rolph Trouillot, *Silencing the Past: Power and the Production of History* (Boston: Beacon Press, 1995).

9   Howard Zinn, *You Can't Be Neutral on a Moving Train: A Personal History of Our Times* (Boston: Beacon Press, 1994), 8.

expensive, inaccessible vanity projects. We still hope to be able to publish the series in isiXhosa and Afrikaans. We have drawn on feedback and reflection on the first series to create what has become this book. Building on our initial goal of speaking to youth in Crossroads and activists across the global south, we hope to now reach an even wider audience to engage in the urgencies of grappling with unfinished histories of struggle at a crucial crossroads today.

Koni Benson
Cape Town
August 11, 2020

Chapter One

Segregation at a Crossroads

ALMOST HALF THE PEOPLE IN CAPE TOWN TODAY LIVE IN SHACKS.

MOST SHACK DWELLERS ARE BLACK GIRLS AND WOMEN.

AFRICAN WOMEN IN CROSSROADS HAVE SAID THAT THE HISTORY OF SHACK DWELLING IN SOUTH AFRICA IS THE HISTORY OF WOMEN.

UNDER WHITE MINORITY RULE AFRICAN WOMEN HAD NO LEGAL RIGHTS TO LIVE IN THE CITIES. BLACK MEN WERE ALLOWED TO MOVE IF AND WHEN THEIR LABOUR WAS NEEDED IN THE CITIES AND MINES AND ON FARMS. BUT WOMEN WERE FORCED TO STAY IN THE RURAL 'LABOUR RESERVES,' CALLED BANTUSTANS (HOMELANDS). IN THE CITIES AFRICAN MEN WERE CALLED BOYS AND WERE FORCED TO STAY IN SO-CALLED 'BACHELOR HOSTELS,' WHICH JUSTIFIED TREATING THEM AS TEMPORARY RESIDENTS IN 'SOUTH AFRICA' AND PAYING THEM 'BACHELOR WAGES,' WHETHER THEY WERE MARRIED OR NOT.

HANDS OFF CROSS ROADS

WHEN WOMEN CAME TO THE CITIES THEY HAD NOWHERE TO STAY AND SET UP SHACKS ON VACANT LAND. THE APARTHEID STATE VIEWED BLACK WOMEN AS NOTHING MORE THAN 'BIRTH MACHINES,' THEIR ROLE IN SOCIETY REDUCED TO REPLENISHING THE 'LABOUR RESERVES.' THROUGHOUT AFRICA, EUROPEAN COLONIAL AUTHORITIES COMPARED NOTES AND IDENTIFIED A PATTERN: WHEN LARGE NUMBERS OF BLACK WOMEN WERE PRESENT IN THE CITIES, BLACK MEN WERE PRESSURED INTO MAKING CERTAIN DEMANDS OF THE STATE OR THEIR EMPLOYERS TO PROVIDE THE SAME BASIC SOCIAL SERVICES — WATER, SANITATION, SCHOOLS, HOSPITALS, ETC. THAT WERE PROVIDED FOR WHITES.

THE TWIN AIMS OF THE GOVERNMENT WERE TO KEEP LABOUR CHEAP AND THE CITIES WHITE; THESE GOALS COULD ONLY BE ACCOMPLISHED BY EXCLUDING BLACK WOMEN FROM THE CITIES.

INFLUX CONTROL WAS A SERIES OF POLICIES DESIGNED TO PLACE SEVERE RESTRICTIONS ON THE MOVEMENT OF BLACKS INTO THE CITIES. PASS LAWS AND RESIDENCY ALLOCATION DICTATED WHO WAS ALLOWED TO STAY IN THE CITY.

INFLUX CONTROL, BIRTH MACHINES, LABOUR RESERVES — THESE WERE THE TERMS USED IN URBAN POLICY AND REFLECTS THE STATE'S VIEW THAT BLACKS WERE LESS THAN HUMAN.

INSTANT LABOUR

10¢

INCIDENTS OF 'SQUATTING' AND ISSUES OVER WHO WAS SETTLING ON WHOSE LAND WERE REPORTED AS EARLY AS THE APPEARANCE OF THE FIRST SETTLERS.

IN 1655 JAN VAN RIEBEECK WROTE IN HIS JOURNAL: ONLY LAST NIGHT IT HAPPENED THAT ABOUT FIFTY OF THESE NATIVES WANTED TO PUT UP THEIR HUTS CLOSE TO THE BANKS OF THE MOAT OF OUR FORTRESS, AND WHEN TOLD IN A FRIENDLY MANNER BY OUR MEN TO GO A LITTLE FARTHER AWAY, THEY DECLARED BOLDLY: 'THIS IS OUR, LAND NOT YOURS. WE WILL PLACE OUR HUTS WHEREVER WE CHOOSE TO.'

WITHIN A FEW YEARS THE SALT AND LIESBEEK RIVERS WERE MARKED AS THE BOUNDARY BETWEEN KHOI, EX-SLAVE AND SETTLER TERRITORIES.

THE NATIONAL PARTY CAME INTO POWER ON A POST-WW2 POLITICAL PLATFORM OF CITIES 'OUT OF CONTROL'. APARTHEID, MEANING 'SEPARATENESS' IN AFRIKAANS, WAS THEIR SOLUTION.

CROSSROADS CAME INTO BEING AS A RESULT OF DISPLACED PEOPLE STANDING THEIR GROUND AND DEMANDING A PLACE TO LIVE IN THE CITY.

AFRICAN WOMEN DEEMED ILLEGAL IN CAPE TOWN WERE AT THE HEART OF CREATING THE PHYSICAL AND SOCIAL INFRASTRUCTURE OF CROSSROADS.

BY THE EARLY 1960S THE APARTHEID STATE HAD SUCCESSFULLY DEMOLISHED THE SELF-MADE COMMUNITIES THEY LABELLED 'SQUATTER CAMPS' OR 'SHANTY TOWNS' THAT MUSHROOMED ACROSS THE PENINSULA IN THE 1940S AND 1950S AND RELOCATED AFRICAN PEOPLE TO THE THREE OFFICIALLY ZONED TOWNSHIPS: LANGA, NYANGA, AND GUGULETHU.

AT THE SAME TIME THE STATE SPENT MILLIONS SUBSIDIZING DEVELOPMENT FOR PEOPLE CLASSIFIED AS WHITE.

THE STATE AIMED TO DISCOURAGE URBAN INFLUX BY CONTINUING TO LIMIT AVAILABLE HOUSING IN THE CITY. HOWEVER, FEWER HOUSES DID NOT TRANSLATE INTO FEWER PEOPLE: IT SIMPLY MEANT OVERCROWDING IN THE OFFICIAL TOWNSHIPS. WOMEN, MIGRANT WORKERS, AND THEIR FAMILIES AS WELL AS WORKERS FROM THE OVERCROWDED STATE-SANCTIONED TOWNSHIPS ESTABLISHED ILLEGAL SETTLEMENTS. BY THE 1970S SQUATTER CAMPS AGAIN DOTTED THE PENINSULA.

Race Determinant Index
(Skin and Hair)

THE APARTHEID STATE SOUGHT NOT ONLY TO DIVIDE BLACK FROM WHITE BUT AFRICAN FROM COLOURED (MIXED RACE). IT FURTHER DIVIDED AFRICANS IN TERMS OF LEGAL AND ILLEGAL WHERE URBAN RIGHTS LIKE ACCOMMODATION WAS CONCERNED, AND PERMANENT (CAPE-BORNER) AND MIGRANT (AMAGODUKA) WHERE EMPLOYMENT WAS CONCERNED.

APARTHEID WAS DESIGNED TO DISORGANIZE AND DIVIDE BLACKS TO CREATE DIFFERENT CHALLENGES, AND COMPETING, SEGREGATED MINORITIES. SUCH DIVIDE-AND-RULE TACTICS JUSTIFIED WHITE MINORITY RULE AND MADE BLACK PEOPLE MORE VULNERABLE TO CONSTANT OPPRESSION THAN A MAJORITY WITH A SHARED SENSE OF DISPOSSESSION AND DISENFRANCHISEMENT.

THE STATE USED AN OPEN FIELD ON THE MARGINS OF THE CITY AS A TEMPORARY TRANSIT CAMP TO DETERMINE WHICH AFRICAN PEOPLE EVICTED FROM COLOURED AREAS HAD LEGAL RIGHTS TO THE CITY AND WHICH WOULD BE DEPORTED TO THE BANTUSTANS.

'LEGALS' WERE GIVEN NOTICE TO MOVE AND SOME WERE EVEN CHAPERONED TO THIS FIELD 'AT THE CROSSROAD.' (WHERE KLIPFONTEIN AND LANSDOWNE ROAD INTERSECT.)

LANSDOWNE RD

KLIPFONTEIN RD

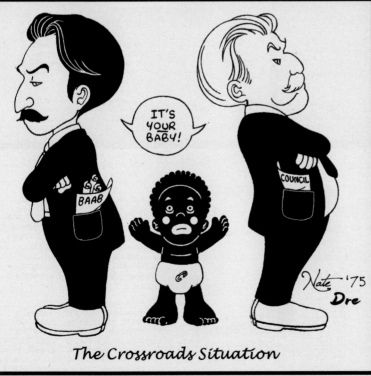

IT'S YOUR BABY!

BAAB

COUNCIL

Nate '75
Dre

The Crossroads Situation

Uncertainty existed over which state body was responsible for the short-sightedly conceived camp. Neither the Bantu Affairs Administration Board (BAAB) nor the Divisional Council wanted the responsibility of Crossroads. Crossroads, technically, was on Divisional Council land but beyond the Eiselen line that separated Coloured from black areas.

BLACK WOMEN CAME TO CROSSROADS FOR ANY OF THE FOLLOWING REASONS:

-THEY FLED TO CROSSROADS TO ESCAPE THE REPEATED DESTRUCTION, BY BULLDOZER, OF HOMES IN SQUATTER CAMPS. (THE WOMEN WOULD ERECT SHACKS, THE AUTHORITIES WOULD DEMOLISH THEIR HOUSES AND DEPORT THEM TO THE BANTUSTANS, THE WOMEN WOULD RETURN, SET UP SHACKS AGAIN, AND THE PROCESS WOULD BEGIN ANEW).

-THEY WERE TIRED OF CONCEALING THEIR ILLEGAL STATUS FROM THE AUTHORITIES: SLEEPING UNDER BEDS IN BACHELOR HOSTELS OR RENTING SPACE IN CONGESTED TOWNSHIPS.

-THEY WERE TIRED OF BEING ARRESTED CONTINUALLY FOR PASS LAW VIOLATIONS. EXPERIENCE TAUGHT THEM THAT THEY WERE LESS LIKELY TO BE HARASSED BY THE AUTHORITIES IN INFORMAL SETTLEMENTS THAN IN THE STATE-SANCTIONED TOWNSHIPS THAT WERE MORE TIGHTLY REGULATED.

-THEY WERE EVICTED FROM NEIGHBOURHOODS SUCH AS RETREAT AND HEATHFIELD (AREAS THAT WERE NOW CLASSIFIED AS COLOURED IN TERMS OF THE GROUP AREAS ACT AND COLOURED LABOUR PREFERENCE POLICY) AND INSTRUCTED TO GO TO CROSSROADS.

-THEY CAME DIRECTLY FROM THE EASTERN CAPE, SEEKING FAMILY, EMPLOYMENT, AND MEDICAL TREATMENT IN CAPE TOWN.

-THEY CAME TO CROSSROADS BECAUSE THEY HAD LOST CHILDREN TO STARVATION IN THE BANTUSTANS AND HAD NO INTENTION OF RETURNING.

Cape Town

CROSSROADS BECAME KNOWN AS 'A PLACE FULL OF TRANSKEI WOMEN.' THIS WAS BECAUSE WOMEN WERE IN CHARGE OF THE MAJORITY OF THE HOUSEHOLDS IN THE CAMP AND HAD NO OTHER OPTIONS OF SHELTER. ADDITIONALLY MEN WORKING IN THE CITY HEARD THAT THERE WAS A PLACE WHERE PEOPLE COULD LIVE AS FAMILIES.

IN SPITE OF THE POLICE RAIDS THAT WOULD FOLLOW, CROSSROADS GREW RAPIDLY. FROM 20 SHACKS HOUSING 100 PEOPLE IN FEBRUARY 1975...

...TO SOMEWHERE BETWEEN 4,000 AND 7,000 PEOPLE LIVING IN 1,017 SHACKS IN APRIL.

IN MARCH 1975, A MONTH AFTER THE FOUNDING OF THE SETTLEMENT, THE FIRST EVICTION NOTICES CAME, AND THE MEN AND WOMEN CREATED SEPARATE COMMITTEES TO DEAL WITH THE THREAT.

THE INCREASINGLY BOLD LEADERSHIP ROLE OF THE WOMEN IN THE CAMP RAISED SOME EYEBROWS.

IN ADDITION TO SEEKING THE ADVICE OF THE BLACK SASH (A LIBERAL ORGANIZATION UNIQUE, AT THE TIME, IN ITS CONCERN FOR THE INDIVIDUAL RIGHTS OF URBAN AFRICAN WOMEN) THE WOMEN FORMED A DELEGATION TO APPROACH THE LOCAL BANTU AFFAIRS COMMISSIONER.

WE COULD NOT TAKE THESE NOTICES SERIOUSLY BECAUSE WE HAD BEEN TOLD BY SOME OTHER INSPECTORS TO COME HERE. WHEN THE NOTICES EXPIRED, THE INSPECTORS ARRIVED AND SAID THEY WOULD PROCEED WITH DEMOLITION. THIS HAPPENED TO THREE WOMEN. AFTER THAT WE CAME TOGETHER AND DECIDED TO TAKE UP THE ISSUE WITH BANTU AFFAIRS IN OBSERVATORY. WE WERE A GROUP OF 58 WOMEN.

AT THIS MEETING THE WOMEN WERE INFORMED THAT CROSSROADS, LIKE ALL AFRICAN SQUATTER CAMPS IN CAPE TOWN, WOULD HAVE TO BE DEMOLISHED, AND BETWEEN FEBRUARY AND APRIL 431 MEN AND 931 WOMEN WERE PROSECUTED FOR BEING IN THE AREA ILLEGALLY.

A PRESS STATEMENT BY THE CROSSROADS WOMEN'S COMMITTEE READ AS FOLLOWS: "WE ARE RESISTING BECAUSE THE INSPECTOR SAID: 'THIS IS YOUR AREA.' THE (DIVISIONAL) COUNCIL TOOK THE PEOPLE WHO WERE STAYING AMONG COLOURED PEOPLE AND BROUGHT THEM HERE. IT IS BECAUSE WE HAVE NO PLACE...THERE WAS EVEN A WHITE INSPECTOR WHO TOLD US TO GO TO CROSSROADS."

THE INJUSTICE OF YET ANOTHER FORCED REMOVAL TARGETING THE MOST VICTIMIZED OF CITY DWELLERS COUPLED WITH THE FACT THAT CROSSROADS WAS NOT WITHIN THE JURISDICTIONAL REACH OF THE BAAB CAPTURED THE INTEREST OF PROGRESSIVE LAWYERS.

SUPPORTED BY CHURCHES SYMPATHETIC TO THE PLIGHT OF THE PEOPLE OF CROSSROADS AND THE BLACK SASH, THE LAWYERS MOUNTED A LEGAL DEFENSE ON BEHALF OF THE CAMP AS A WHOLE.

HAD THE WOMEN NOT COME TOGETHER AND REACHED OUT TO THOSE PROGRESSIVE INDIVIDUALS AND ORGANIZATIONS, CHALLENGING THE STATE THROUGH THE COURTS WOULD NEVER HAVE BEEN UNDERTAKEN OR CONSIDERED POSSIBLE BY WHITE LIBERALS.

WHEN PEOPLE WERE CHARGED WITH TRESPASSING THE COURTS ACTUALLY TOOK THE BAAB EVICTION NOTICES THAT DIRECTED PEOPLE TO CROSSROADS INTO CONSIDERATION AND IN FEBRUARY 1976 RULED IN FAVOUR OF ONE WOMAN'S TEST EVICTION CASE. BAAB WAS NOW FORCED TO ABANDON THE USE OF TRESPASSING AS GROUNDS FOR EVICTION.

IT WAS A MOMENTOUS LEGAL VICTORY.

IN RETALIATION THE STATE CHANGED THE LAW: THE ILLEGAL SQUATTING ACT WAS AMENDED SO THAT THE STATE NO LONGER HAD LEGAL STANDING TO CONTEST SHACK DEMOLITIONS.

THE DIVISIONAL COUNCIL APPLIED TO THE SUPREME COURT TO HAVE CROSSROADS DEMOLISHED, STATING THAT INADEQUATE SERVICES AMOUNTED TO A HEALTH HAZARD. BUT THE CROSSROADS LAWYERS USED A CONTRADICTION IN NEW LEGISLATION THAT SUGGESTED CONCERNS OF HEALTH COULD BE DEALT WITH BY DECLARING AN AREA AN EMERGENCY CAMP INSTEAD OF DEMOLISHING IT.

MR. MDAYI (THE CHAIRMAN OF ONE OF THE TWO MEN'S COMMITTEES) APPLIED FOR CROSSROADS TO BE DECLARED AN EMERGENCY CAMP. ON JUNE 29, 1976, CROSSROADS WAS GIVEN LEGAL STATUS AS AN EMERGENCY CAMP.

THE COUNCIL HAD THEN TO PROVIDE SERVICES SUCH AS WATER, TAPS, REFUSE, AND NIGHT SOIL REMOVAL. A PROPOSAL WAS MADE THAT RESIDENTS PAY R10 PER MONTH AS RENT.

AFTER WINNING THE LEGAL BATTLE IN '76, CROSSROADS ACQUIRED A SEMBLANCE OF OFFICIAL LEGITIMACY. THE LEGAL BATTLE MEANT THAT CROSSROADS WOULD GAIN SOME SERVICES AND BE FREE OF THE THREAT OF DEMOLITION, BUT IT DID NOT MEAN THAT INDIVIDUALS LIVING THERE WOULD BE GIVEN THE RIGHT TO REMAIN IN THE CITY. MOBILIZING AND ALLIANCES WITH OUTSIDE ORGANIZATIONS CONTINUED BECAUSE INDIVIDUALS WERE STILL HARASSED FOR PASSES, ARRESTED, AND DEPORTED.

2302

BY 1978 CROSSROADS WAS THE ONLY REMAINING INFORMAL SETTLEMENT FOR AFRICAN PEOPLE IN THE CAPE PENINSULA.

AFTER TWO YEARS OF EVADING THE REACH OF THE BANTU AUTHORITY BY MEANS OF THE EMERGENCY CAMP ACT, CROSSROADS GRABBED THE STATE'S ATTENTION. MANY REFUGEES HAD FLED THERE FROM OTHER DEMOLITIONS. AFTER MODDERDAM WAS DEMOLISHED PIK BOTHA TOLD THE PRESS:

CROSSROADS WILL HAVE TO BE DEMOLISHED, LIKE ALL OTHER SQUATTER CAMPS.

IN THE FACE OF THIS INTENSIFIED STATE CAMPAIGN TO DESTROY THEIR HOMES AND COMMUNITY THE WOMEN'S COMMITTEE TOOK THE LEAD TO ORGANIZE A POWERFUL MOVEMENT TO DEFY THE APARTHEID REGIME AND DEFEND CROSSROADS. IN THE EARLY YEARS THEY PUSHED BOUNDARIES: FROM INDIVIDUAL RESISTANCE IN THE 1960S TO BEING ORGANIZED AS A COLLECTIVE IN THE EARLY 1970S. AFTER 1978 THEIR PROTESTS WOULD BECOME OVERTLY POLITICAL AND HIGHLY PUBLICIZED. WOMEN DECIDED THAT THE BEST WAY TO WITHSTAND REMOVAL WAS TO EXTEND THEIR ALLIANCES AND ORGANIZE A HIGHLY VISIBLE PUBLIC CAMPAIGN AT THE LOCAL, NATIONAL AND INTERNATIONAL LEVEL. THE AIM WAS TO CALL ATTENTION TO THEIR PLIGHT.

THEIR SOLIDARITY NETWORK WAS BUILT ON EARLIER RELATIONSHIPS WITH ANTI-APARTHEID ACTIVISTS AND ORGANIZATIONS LIKE THE BLACK SASH, CHURCHES, UNIVERSITY STUDENTS, LAWYERS, AND HUMAN RIGHTS ASSOCIATIONS. THEIR MANY PROTEST ACTIONS CAPTURED THE ATTENTION OF POWERFUL FORCES WITHIN SOUTH AFRICA: FROM GOVERNMENT TO BUSINESS, TO THE INTERNATIONAL COMMUNITY, WHICH WAS THREATENING THE COUNTRY WITH SANCTIONS.

ON JUNE 5, 1978, BAAB OFFICIALS SURROUNDED CROSSROADS AND STARTED ARRESTING RESIDENTS AND SHOOTING TEAR GAS, WHILE PEOPLE TRIED TO MAKE THEIR WAY TO WORK. THUS BEGAN A NEW WAVE OF RAIDS WHICH BECAME AN ALMOST DAILY OCCURRENCE.

BY 1978 THERE WERE 9,000 CHILDREN IN CROSSROADS ATTENDING THE TWO HANDMADE SCHOOLS ORGANIZED BY WOMEN LEADERS. THESE SCHOOL BUILDINGS WERE ALSO USED AS COMMUNITY HALLS FOR POLITICAL, CULTURAL, AND RELIGIOUS GATHERINGS AND WOMEN WERE PREPARED TO DEFEND THEM AT ANY COST.

WHEN 600 RIOT POLICE INVADED SIZAMILE SCHOOL LOCAL WOMEN RESISTED AND 300 WERE ARRESTED.

TWO DAYS LATER CROSSROADS WOMEN STAGED A MASS ACTION WHEREBY BETWEEN 200 AND 300 OF THEM ARRIVED AT THE BAAB OFFICES IN GOODWOOD BEFORE DAWN, STANDING SILENT WITH BABIES ON THEIR BACKS READY TO MEET MUNICIPAL WORKERS ARRIVING AT WORK.

LANDDROSHOWE
GOODWOOD
MAGISTRATE COURTS

NONTOZAMA STUURMAN

WE NEVER SLEPT ON THAT DAY. A PERSON WHO DID NOT HAVE A CHILD WOULD PUT ANOTHER PERSON'S CHILD ON HER BACK.

WHEN THE GOVERNMENT OFFICIALS CAME, THEY SAID WHAT'S GOING ON?

BECAUSE THE OFFICIALS REFUSED TO COME OUTSIDE, THE WOMEN RELUCTANTLY AGREED TO SEVEN REPRESENTATIVES GOING INSIDE THE OFFICES. THEY DEMANDED AN EXPLANATION FOR THE DESTRUCTION OF THE SCHOOL AND THE HARASSMENT THEY SUFFERED. THEY REJECTED THE STATE'S OFFER OF NEW HOUSING DEVELOPMENTS IN THE TRANSKEI. THE AUTHORITIES INSTRUCTED THEM NOT TO DEMONSTRATE OR TALK TO REPORTERS. THEY INFORMED THE WOMEN TO WRITE LETTERS AND MAKE APPOINTMENTS IN THE FUTURE. THEY WERE TOLD TO RETURN ON JUNE 17, FOR QUESTIONING SUPPOSEDLY.

THE WOMEN WOULD LIKELY HAVE BEEN ARRESTED HAD THEY RETURNED. INSTEAD, THEY IMMEDIATELY WENT TO THE PRESS. THEY TOLD THE NEWSPAPERS THAT THEY HAD NOTHING TO LOSE. IN FACT THEY BELIEVED THAT PUBLICITY AFFORDED THE BEST PROTECTION AGAINST DEMOLITION.

THE ARGUS NEWSPAPER NOTED: EACH WOMAN WHO TOLD HER STORY ENDED ON THE SAME NOTE:

IF I HAVE ANY RIGHTS, LET ME HAVE THEM IN CROSSROADS!

IF I HAVE ANY RIGHTS, LET ME HAVE THEM IN CROSSROADS!

IF I HAVE ANY RIGHTS, LET ME HAVE THEM IN CROSSROADS!

IF I HAVE ANY RIGHTS, LET ME HAVE THEM IN CROSSROADS!

Chapter Two

I Took Out the Loudhailer

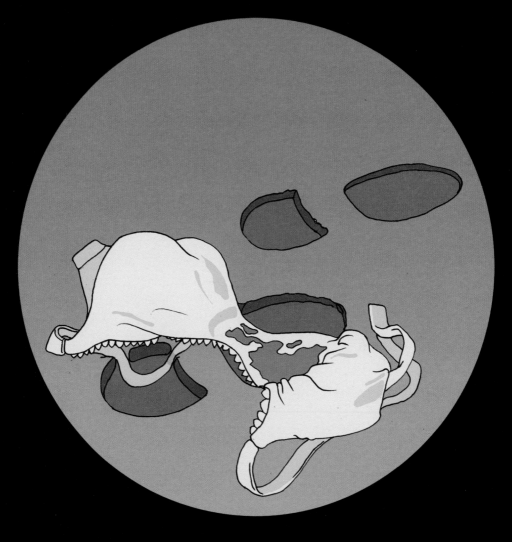

MEMBERS OF THE CROSSROADS WOMEN'S COMMITTEE REPRESENTED THE DIVERSE BACKGROUNDS, EXPERIENCES, AND SOCIAL POSITIONS OF WOMEN IN THE CAMP.

SOME COMMITTEE WOMEN WERE WIDOWED, DIVORCED, OR SINGLE MOTHERS; SOME WERE MARRIED WITH THEIR HUSBANDS INVOLVED IN POLITICS, SOME WITH PARTNERS WHO WERE UNCOMFORTABLE WITH THE IDEA OF WOMEN IN POLITICAL LEADERSHIP ROLES.

SOME WERE ARTICULATE AND EXPERIENCED TEACHERS, SOME SPOKE MANY LANGUAGES IN ADDITION TO ISIXHOSA, SOME WERE OLDER WOMEN WHO COULD NOT READ OR WRITE AND SPOKE ALMOST NO ENGLISH AT ALL, SOME WERE ENTREPRENEURS, AND SOME WERE YOUNG MOTHERS.

THEY USED A RANGE OF TERMS TO DESCRIBE THEMSELVES: BUSINESSWOMEN; 'ILLITERATE,' TEACHERS, AND 'NEVER MIND YOU MARRIED OR NOT.'

THEY USED THEIR VOICES AS A SHARP WEAPON AGAINST APARTHEID, CEMENTING A HISTORY AND ARTICULATING THE VISION OF THEIR STRUGGLE TO THE LOCAL PRESS AND THE INTERNATIONAL LEFT.

REGINA
NTONGANA

JOHNSON
NGXOBONGWANA

TO BETTER ORGANIZE THE DEFENSE OF THE CAMP, THE WOMEN'S COMMITTEE ELECTED A SECRETARY AND TREASURER.

MRS. NTONGANA WAS ASKED TO GIVE UP HER JOB AT A RESTAURANT IN TOWN TO DEVOTE HERSELF FULL-TIME TO THE COMMITTEE AND HOLD THE POSITION OF CHAIR.

JOHNSON NGXOBONGWANA, LIKEWISE, WAS ALSO ASKED TO QUIT HIS JOB AND TO BECOME THE FULL-TIME CHAIR OF ONE OF THE MEN'S COMMITTEES, THE NOXOLO SCHOOL COMMITTEE. HE WAS ARTICULATE AND A CRITICAL THINKER BUT HIS LEADERSHIP STYLE WOULD GRADUALLY BECOME AUTOCRATIC.

THE WAYS IN WHICH THE COMMITTEES WORKED AND THE ISSUES THAT THEY FOCUSED ON WERE HIGHLY GENDERED.

THE MEN'S COMMITTEES FOCUSED ON SECURITY AND LAW AND ORDER, WHILE THE WOMEN FOCUSED ON EDUCATION, HEALTH, WATER SUPPLIES, AND SANITATION.

THE LEADERSHIP ROLE OF THE WOMEN WAS NOT SOMETHING THAT THE MEN READILY ACCEPTED.

ACCORDING TO MRS. NTONGANA:
'THEY HAD THIS CUSTOM, THEY DIDN'T ACCEPT THAT A WOMAN SHOULD BE SO ACTIVE. THEY SOMETIMES TAKE IT BUT DID NOT LIKE IT, BECAUSE IT IS THE CUSTOM OF OUR PEOPLE THAT THE WOMEN STAYS IN THE KITCHEN. THE WOMEN CAN'T BE IN THE FRONTLINE. SOMETIMES IT WAS HURTING THEM, IT WAS NOT VERY NICE.'

DESPITE THESE CONFLICTS, AN INTERIM JOINT COMMITTEE BETWEEN THE WOMEN'S AND THE NOXOLO AND SIZAMILE COMMITTEES WAS FORMED IN 1978 TO COORDINATE WITH OUTSIDE ALLIANCES AGAINST THE THREAT OF FORCED REMOVAL.

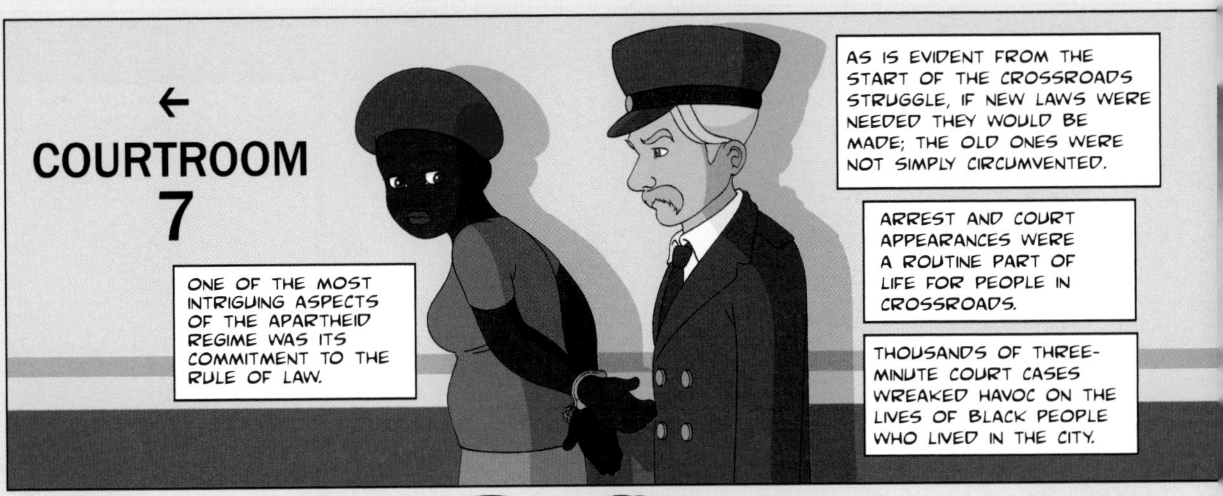
← COURTROOM 7
ONE OF THE MOST INTRIGUING ASPECTS OF THE APARTHEID REGIME WAS ITS COMMITMENT TO THE RULE OF LAW.
AS IS EVIDENT FROM THE START OF THE CROSSROADS STRUGGLE, IF NEW LAWS WERE NEEDED THEY WOULD BE MADE; THE OLD ONES WERE NOT SIMPLY CIRCUMVENTED.
ARREST AND COURT APPEARANCES WERE A ROUTINE PART OF LIFE FOR PEOPLE IN CROSSROADS.
THOUSANDS OF THREE-MINUTE COURT CASES WREAKED HAVOC ON THE LIVES OF BLACK PEOPLE WHO LIVED IN THE CITY.

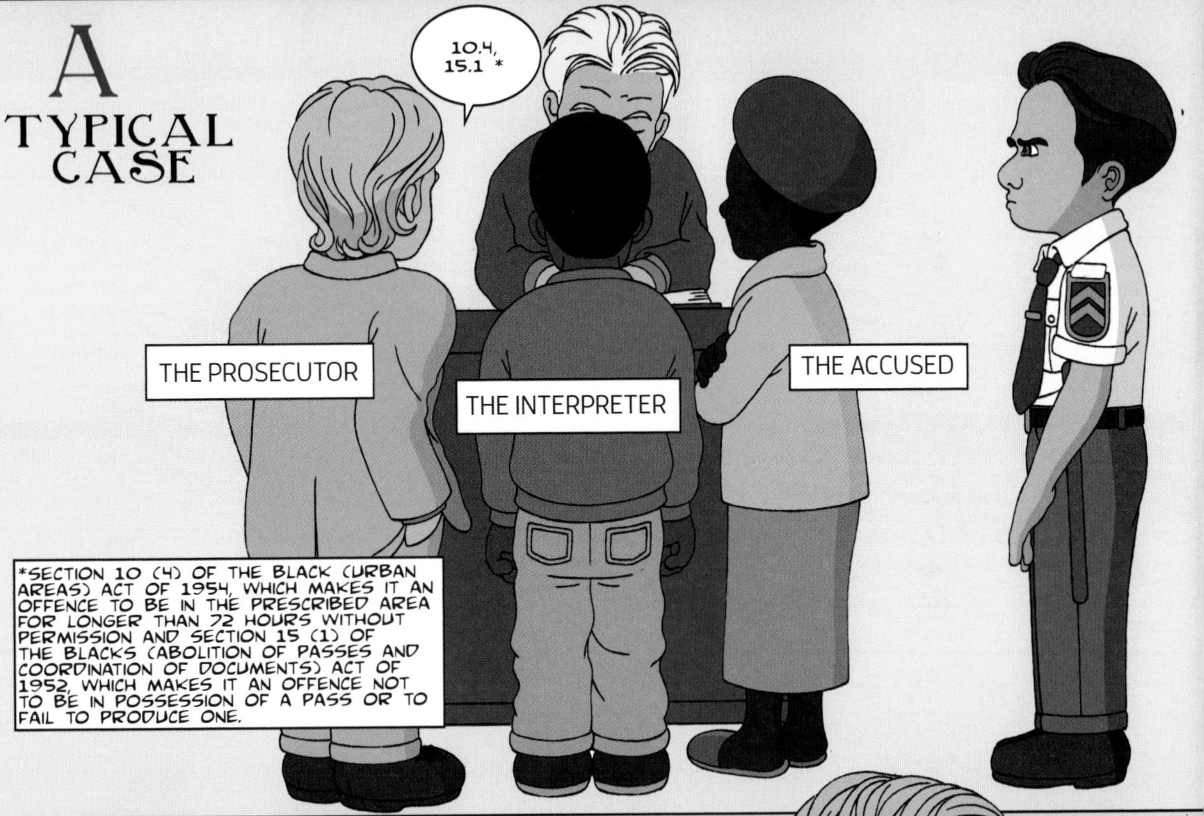
A TYPICAL CASE
10.4, 15.1 *
THE PROSECUTOR
THE INTERPRETER
THE ACCUSED
*SECTION 10 (4) OF THE BLACK (URBAN AREAS) ACT OF 1954, WHICH MAKES IT AN OFFENCE TO BE IN THE PRESCRIBED AREA FOR LONGER THAN 72 HOURS WITHOUT PERMISSION AND SECTION 15 (1) OF THE BLACKS (ABOLITION OF PASSES AND COORDINATION OF DOCUMENTS) ACT OF 1952, WHICH MAKES IT AN OFFENCE NOT TO BE IN POSSESSION OF A PASS OR TO FAIL TO PRODUCE ONE.

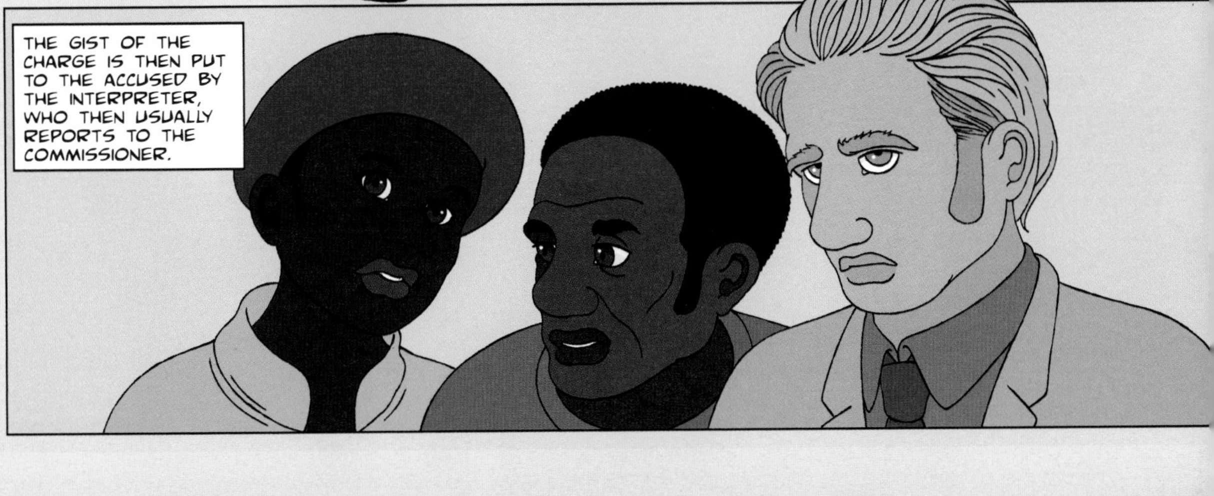
THE GIST OF THE CHARGE IS THEN PUT TO THE ACCUSED BY THE INTERPRETER, WHO THEN USUALLY REPORTS TO THE COMMISSIONER.

THE NAME OF THE NEXT ACCUSED IS USUALLY CALLED BEFORE SENTENCE IS PASSED AND A RAPID PROCESSION ENSUES. THE ACCUSED HAS A CHANCE TO PAY THE FINE IMMEDIATELY, OTHERWISE THE PRISON SENTENCE BEGINS AT POLLSMOOR

IN THE LATE 1970S THE AVERAGE FINE OF R70 REPRESENTED APPROXIMATELY TWO TO THREE WEEKS' WAGES FOR UNSKILLED WORKERS.

THE STATE COLLECTED AN INCREDIBLE AMOUNT OF MONEY FROM PEOPLE WITHOUT MONEY. FROM A TOTAL OF R150,000 COLLECTED FROM PASS LAW FINES IN 1979, TO R283,576 IN 1981.

THE WESTERN CAPE WAS ALWAYS A TEST GROUND FOR NEW PASS LAWS AND BYLAWS. ALTHOUGH AFRICAN PEOPLE WERE NOT A MAJORITY IN CAPE TOWN, THE PERCENTAGE OF PASS LAW PROSECUTIONS, OF HARASSMENT, WERE HIGHER THAN ANYWHERE IN SOUTH AFRICA.

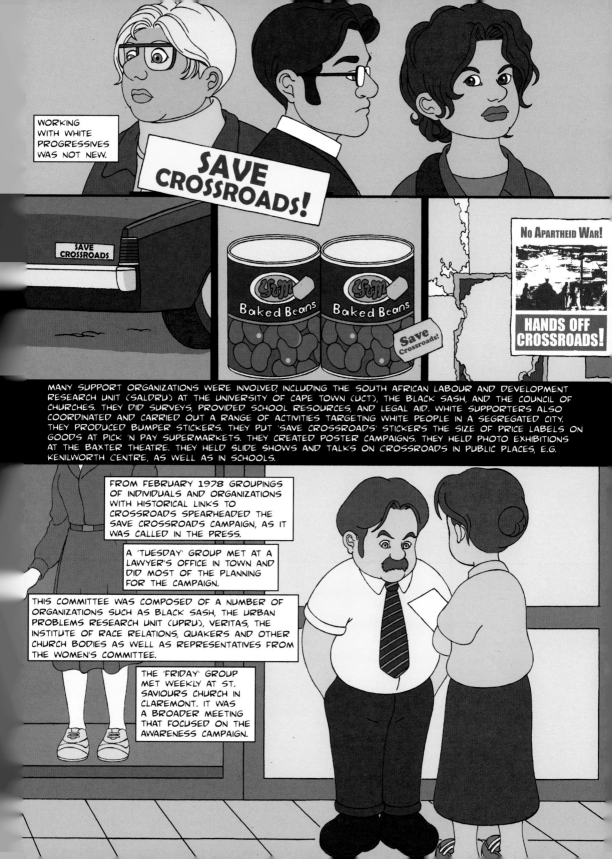

WORKING WITH WHITE PROGRESSIVES WAS NOT NEW.

SAVE CROSSROADS!

SAVE CROSSROADS

Baked Beans

Baked Beans

Save Crossroads!

No Apartheid War!

HANDS OFF CROSSROADS!

MANY SUPPORT ORGANIZATIONS WERE INVOLVED, INCLUDING THE SOUTH AFRICAN LABOUR AND DEVELOPMENT RESEARCH UNIT (SALDRU) AT THE UNIVERSITY OF CAPE TOWN (UCT), THE BLACK SASH, AND THE COUNCIL OF CHURCHES. THEY DID SURVEYS, PROVIDED SCHOOL RESOURCES, AND LEGAL AID. WHITE SUPPORTERS ALSO COORDINATED AND CARRIED OUT A RANGE OF ACTIVITIES TARGETING WHITE PEOPLE IN A SEGREGATED CITY. THEY PRODUCED BUMPER STICKERS. THEY PUT 'SAVE CROSSROADS' STICKERS THE SIZE OF PRICE LABELS ON GOODS AT PICK 'N PAY SUPERMARKETS. THEY CREATED POSTER CAMPAIGNS. THEY HELD PHOTO EXHIBITIONS AT THE BAXTER THEATRE. THEY HELD SLIDE SHOWS AND TALKS ON CROSSROADS IN PUBLIC PLACES, E.G. KENILWORTH CENTRE, AS WELL AS IN SCHOOLS.

FROM FEBRUARY 1978 GROUPINGS OF INDIVIDUALS AND ORGANIZATIONS WITH HISTORICAL LINKS TO CROSSROADS SPEARHEADED THE SAVE CROSSROADS CAMPAIGN, AS IT WAS CALLED IN THE PRESS.

A 'TUESDAY' GROUP MET AT A LAWYER'S OFFICE IN TOWN AND DID MOST OF THE PLANNING FOR THE CAMPAIGN.

THIS COMMITTEE WAS COMPOSED OF A NUMBER OF ORGANIZATIONS SUCH AS BLACK SASH, THE URBAN PROBLEMS RESEARCH UNIT (UPRU), VERITAS, THE INSTITUTE OF RACE RELATIONS, QUAKERS AND OTHER CHURCH BODIES AS WELL AS REPRESENTATIVES FROM THE WOMEN'S COMMITTEE.

THE 'FRIDAY' GROUP MET WEEKLY AT ST. SAVIOURS CHURCH IN CLAREMONT. IT WAS A BROADER MEETING THAT FOCUSED ON THE AWARENESS CAMPAIGN.

A DAY OF PRAYER AND INTERNATIONAL SOLIDARITY WAS CELEBRATED IN CROSSROADS AND IN CITIES AND CHURCHES THE WORLD OVER, ON SUNDAY, JULY 30, 1978.

THE DIVISION OF LABOUR, HOWEVER, DID NOT GO UNQUESTIONED.

AT ONE MEETING A FIELD WORKER FOR THE SA INSTITUTE OF RACE RELATIONS QUESTIONED THE LACK OF INVOLVEMENT OF PEOPLE FROM CROSSROADS AT THESE ACTIVITIES.

WALLACE MGOQI, A VERITAS WORKER IN CROSSROADS, REPLIED:

THE CROSSROADS COMMITTEE HAS SANCTIONED ALL AND ANY EFFORTS ON THE PART OF CONCERNED CITIZENS TO SUPPORT THE FURTHERING OF THE STAY OF DEMOLITION. THERE IS OFTEN DIFFICULTY WITH TRANSPORT WHICH MAKES PARTICIPATION IN PROJECTS OUTSIDE THE COMMUNITY DIFFICULT. THERE IS, OF COURSE, ALSO FEAR OF EXPOSURE.

ONE LETTER FROM CROSSROADS TO THIS NETWORK OF WHITE LIBERALS SAID: 'WE BLACK PEOPLE OF CROSSROADS APPEAL TO YOU WHITE PEOPLE TO TAKE UP OUR CASE WITH YOUR LEADERS, BECAUSE WE BLACK

CROSSROADS BECAME THE FOCUS OF BOTH THE WHITE HARDLINERS (VERKRAMPTES) AND REFORMERS (VERLIGTES) AT THE HIGHEST LEVEL OF STATE: BOTH ACKNOWLEDGED THE NEED FOR AN IMMEDIATE AND DECISIVE RESPONSE TO CROSSROADS, A SYMBOL OF THE LARGER APARTHEID PROJECT IN CRISIS.

POWER POLITICS HAD COME TO A HEAD AND THE REFORMERS AND CONSERVATIVES WITHIN THE NATIONAL PARTY WERE VYING FOR AUTHORITY.

CROSSROADS HAD COME TO SYMBOLIZE THE DIRECTION OF LABOUR POLICIES IN THE CAPE.

CONSERVATIVES CARRIED OUT TWO BRUTAL RAIDS IN THE LEAD-UP TO WHAT THEY PLANNED AS THE FINAL DEMOLITION OF CROSSROADS SET FOR NOVEMBER 1978.

ON THE 6TH OF SEPTEMBER THE CAMP WAS SURROUNDED AND RAIDED, WITH OVER 450 ARRESTED AND 58 CHARGED.

THE STATE JUSTIFIED THE RAID ON THE GROUNDS THAT PEOPLE WERE 'HARBOURING ILLEGALS' IN CROSSROADS.

DESPITE THE NATIONAL AND INTERNATIONAL OUTCRY OVER CROSSROADS, THE CONSERVATIVES, STRUGGLING FOR STATE CONTROL, MANDATED A SECOND 'CRIME PREVENTION' RAID OF CROSSROADS ON SEPTEMBER 15, 1978.

HUNDREDS OF PEOPLE WERE ARRESTED, MANY INJURED, THREE WERE SHOT AND ONE PERSON, SINDILE NDLELA, WAS KILLED.

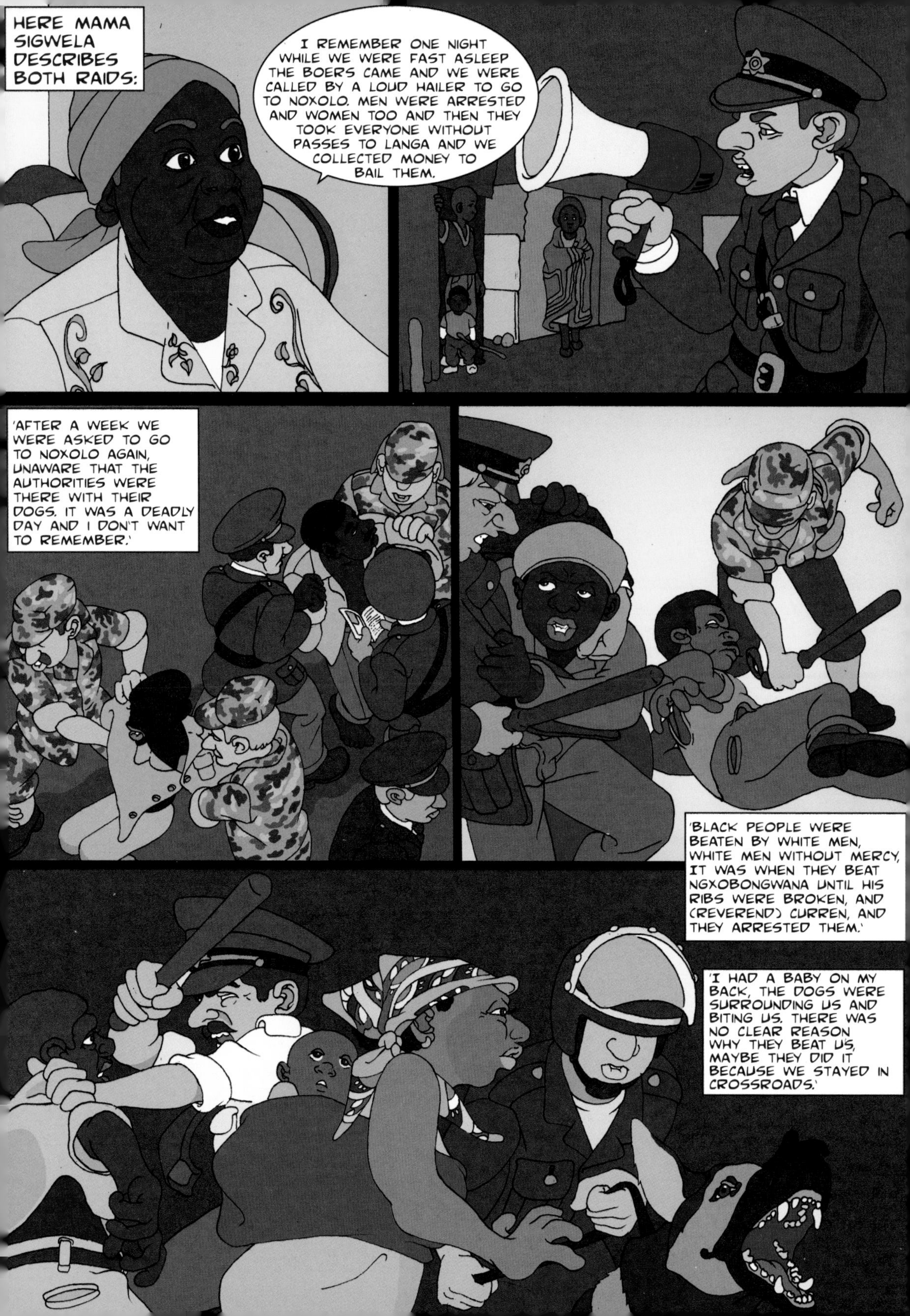
HERE MAMA SIGWELA DESCRIBES BOTH RAIDS:
I REMEMBER ONE NIGHT WHILE WE WERE FAST ASLEEP THE BOERS CAME AND WE WERE CALLED BY A LOUD HAILER TO GO TO NOXOLO. MEN WERE ARRESTED AND WOMEN TOO AND THEN THEY TOOK EVERYONE WITHOUT PASSES TO LANGA AND WE COLLECTED MONEY TO BAIL THEM.
'AFTER A WEEK WE WERE ASKED TO GO TO NOXOLO AGAIN, UNAWARE THAT THE AUTHORITIES WERE THERE WITH THEIR DOGS. IT WAS A DEADLY DAY AND I DON'T WANT TO REMEMBER.'
'BLACK PEOPLE WERE BEATEN BY WHITE MEN, WHITE MEN WITHOUT MERCY, IT WAS WHEN THEY BEAT NGXOBONGWANA UNTIL HIS RIBS WERE BROKEN, AND (REVEREND) CURREN, AND THEY ARRESTED THEM.'
'I HAD A BABY ON MY BACK, THE DOGS WERE SURROUNDING US AND BITING US. THERE WAS NO CLEAR REASON WHY THEY BEAT US, MAYBE THEY DID IT BECAUSE WE STAYED IN CROSSROADS.'

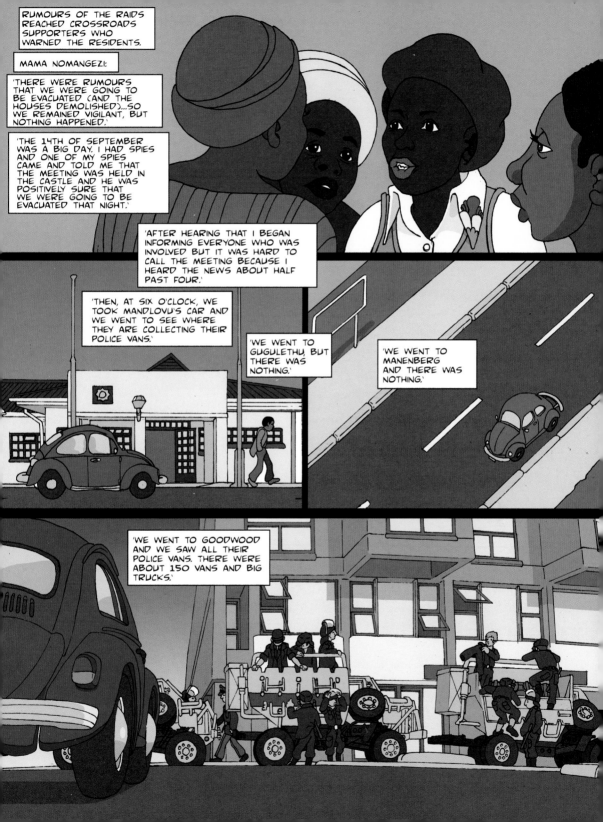

RUMOURS OF THE RAIDS REACHED CROSSROADS SUPPORTERS WHO WARNED THE RESIDENTS.

MAMA NOMANGEZI:

'THERE WERE RUMOURS THAT WE WERE GOING TO BE EVACUATED (AND THE HOUSES DEMOLISHED)...SO WE REMAINED VIGILANT, BUT NOTHING HAPPENED.'

'THE 14TH OF SEPTEMBER WAS A BIG DAY. I HAD SPIES AND ONE OF MY SPIES CAME AND TOLD ME THAT THE MEETING WAS HELD IN THE CASTLE AND HE WAS POSITIVELY SURE THAT WE WERE GOING TO BE EVACUATED THAT NIGHT.'

'AFTER HEARING THAT I BEGAN INFORMING EVERYONE WHO WAS INVOLVED BUT IT WAS HARD TO CALL THE MEETING BECAUSE I HEARD THE NEWS ABOUT HALF PAST FOUR.'

'THEN, AT SIX O'CLOCK, WE TOOK MANDLOVU'S CAR AND WE WENT TO SEE WHERE THEY ARE COLLECTING THEIR POLICE VANS.'

'WE WENT TO GUGULETHU, BUT THERE WAS NOTHING.'

'WE WENT TO MANENBERG AND THERE WAS NOTHING.'

'WE WENT TO GOODWOOD AND WE SAW ALL THEIR POLICE VANS. THERE WERE ABOUT 150 VANS AND BIG TRUCKS.'

'THE PEOPLE WERE ALSO THERE AND IT WAS EASY FOR US TO CONFIRM THAT THEY WERE REALLY COMING FOR US TODAY. LUCKILY, I HAD A LOUDHAILER IN THE CAR. MRS. MAPISA AND I, MANDLOVU WERE IN THE CAR (BUT I CAN'T REMEMBER EVERYONE). I TOOK OUT THE LOUDHAILER AND I TOLD PEOPLE TO BE ON ALERT BECAUSE THE POLICE WERE COMING.'

'I WENT BACK AND CALLED FOR ALL WOMEN TO COME TO MY HOUSE.'

'WE ARE GOING TO FIGHT TODAY... BECAUSE WE'VE GOT NOWHERE TO GO.'

'THE POLICE ARRIVED AT ELEVEN O' CLOCK.'

'IT WAS A BIG FIGHT BETWEEN THE PEOPLE AND THE POLICE. WE HEARD THAT THEY WERE COMING TO DEMOLISH BUT THEY DIDN'T COME TO DEMOLISH. THEY CAME TO FIGHT BECAUSE NOT EVEN A SINGLE HOUSE WAS DEMOLISHED THAT DAY.'

'THE ONLY THING THEY DID WAS TO STRIP PEOPLE. IT WAS LIKE A WAR. THE NEXT MORNING THEY SHOT MR. NDLELA AND THEY TRIED TO DRAG HIM BUT THE PEOPLE ALSO TRIED TO DRAG HIM TO THEIR SIDE.'

THAT AFTERNOON THE WOMEN'S COMMITTEE LED TWENTY WOMEN TO MARCH ON THE COURTS IN LANGA, SAYING THEY WANTED TO BE ARRESTED TOO.

MAMA NTONGANA:

THE MEN DID NOTHING TO DESERVE BEING ARRESTED. NEITHER DID WE, SO WE WANTED THE POLICE TO ARREST US TOO.

THE WOMEN'S COMMITTEE PUT OUT A PUBLIC STATEMENT ON 15 SEPTEMBER AND TWO DAYS LATER THE JOINT COMMITTEE PUBLICIZED THEIR STATEMENT TO THE POLICE COMMISSIONER.

A FEW DAYS AFTER THE RAID, TWENTY-TWO MEMBERS OF THE HOUSE OF REPRESENTATIVES IN THE UNITED STATES APPEALED TO PRESIDENT CARTER TO INTERVENE DIPLOMATICALLY TO DISCOURAGE THE S.A. GOVERNMENT FROM ATTACKING CROSSROADS.

POLITICAL DISPUTES PEAKED IN THE MEDIA FOLLOWING THE RAID:

The Washington Post

September 20, 1978

'BY AUTHORIZING THE POLICE RAIDS ON CROSSROADS, PRIME MINISTER VORSTER IS CLEARLY TELLING THE WORLD THAT HE HAS LITTLE REGARD FOR THE HUMAN RIGHTS OF MILLIONS OF SOUTH AFRICANS UNDER THE RULE OF APARTHEID.'

SOUTH AFRICAN MINISTER OF POLICE, JIMMY KRUGER: 'THE UNITED STATES HAS NOT REACTED VERY QUICKLY WHEN THE RHODESIAN VISCOUNT WAS SHOT DOWN BY A TERRORIST RECENTLY, BUT LET A SOUTH AFRICAN POLICEMEN DRAW HIS BATON AND A HULLABALOO IS CREATED OVERSEAS.'

CAPE TIMES

August 28, 1978

THE CAPE TIMES EDITOR, TONY HEARD: 'CROSSROADS HIGHLIGHTS EVERY ONE OF THE POLITICAL AND SOCIAL FEATURES OF A SOUTH AFRICAN WAY OF LIFE THAT HAS LEFT THIS COUNTRY FRIENDLESS, DISLIKED AND DISTRUSTED, FACING MOUNTING ANIMOSITY BEYOND OUR BORDERS AND A GROWING HOSTILITY FROM THE VOTELESS 20 MILLION

BEYOND MORALITY, CROSSROADS FED INTO INTERNATIONAL DIVESTMENT CAMPAIGNS, WHICH HAD A DETRIMENTAL EFFECT ON THE ECONOMY AND PLAYED AN IMPORTANT ROLE IN REFORMERS' DECISION TO NEGOTIATE A SETTLEMENT WITH THE 'VOTELESS' IN CROSSROADS.

MONOPOLY CAPITAL HAD TAKEN AN INTEREST IN THE CROSSROADS SITUATION FOR SOME TIME AND IN 1978 THE URBAN FOUNDATION INTERVENED DIRECTLY WITH THE AIM OF FINDING A SOLUTION TO THE CROSSROADS CONFLICT.

THE URBAN FOUNDATION WAS FORMED IN 1977 UNDER THE SPONSORSHIP OF 150 BUSINESSES AND REPRESENTED LOCAL CAPITAL INTERESTS WHICH SAW CROSSROADS AND ANTI-APARTHEID RESISTANCE AS A MAJOR THREAT TO ECONOMIC AND POLITICAL STABILITY.

IN THE LATE 1970S CALLS FOR MARKET LIBERALIZATION WERE ON THE RISE AS A CAPITALIST SOLUTION TO SAVE A SYSTEM IN CRISIS IN SOUTH AFRICA.

Mr. Phiri's X-RAY'S

REMOVING OBSTACLES TO THE EXPLOITATION OF THE MARKET FORCES WAS THE GOAL OF THE URBAN FOUNDATION AND DEPOLITICIZING MEASURES OF CONTROL WAS KEY.

FOLLOWING THE EXAMPLE OF USAID, LOCAL CAPITAL DECIDED TO INVEST IN THE WINNING HORSE AND BEGAN TO LOOK TO STEER THE ANTI-APARTHEID STRUGGLE AWAY FROM SOCIALISM.

IT HAS BEEN ARGUED THAT THE DEPOLITICIZATION OF QUESTIONS CONCERNING POVERTY, URBANIZATION, AND LIVING CONDITIONS IN GENERAL REFLECTED A WIDER ESTABLISHMENT CONSENSUS AND HAD MORE TO DO WITH SAVING CAPITALISM AND LITTLE TO DO WITH GIVING UP ON THE RACISM OF APARTHEID.

Chapter Three

Imfuduso

THE SHOCK OF THE SEPTEMBER 1978 RAID LEFT MOST CROSSROADS RESIDENTS AND THEIR ALLIES IN THE SAVE CROSSROADS CAMPAIGN DEPLETED.

AFTER SUCH AN INTENSIVE CAMPAIGN IT APPEARED THAT IN FACT HARDLINERS IN THE STATE WOULD HAVE THEIR WAY AND DEMOLISH THE CAMP LIKE ALL OTHER AFRICAN INFORMAL SETTLEMENTS IN THE CITY.

BUT THE RAID HAD BEEN PLANNED BY THE EXTREMELY CONSERVATIVE SECTOR OF THE STATE (VERKRAMPTES) SPECIFICALLY AT A TIME WHEN THE MINISTERIAL POST RESPONSIBLE FOR 'URBAN NATIVES' WAS VACANT BECAUSE OF THE INTENSIFYING DEBATES WITHIN GOVERNMENT ABOUT HOW TO RESPOND TO RECESSION AND TO THE PROTESTS AND DIVESTMENT CAMPAIGNS HURTING SOUTH AFRICAN ECONOMIC AND SOCIAL STABILITY.

IN THE END, PIET KOORNHOF, A VERLIGTE(REFORMER) WAS APPOINTED AND HE DECIDED THAT SOLVING THE CROSSROADS PROBLEM WOULD BE HIS BABY.

THE WOMEN'S COMMITTEE, MEANWHILE, HAD CHANNELED THE TRAUMA OF THE RECENT RAID INTO THE CREATION OF A THEATRICAL PRODUCTION.

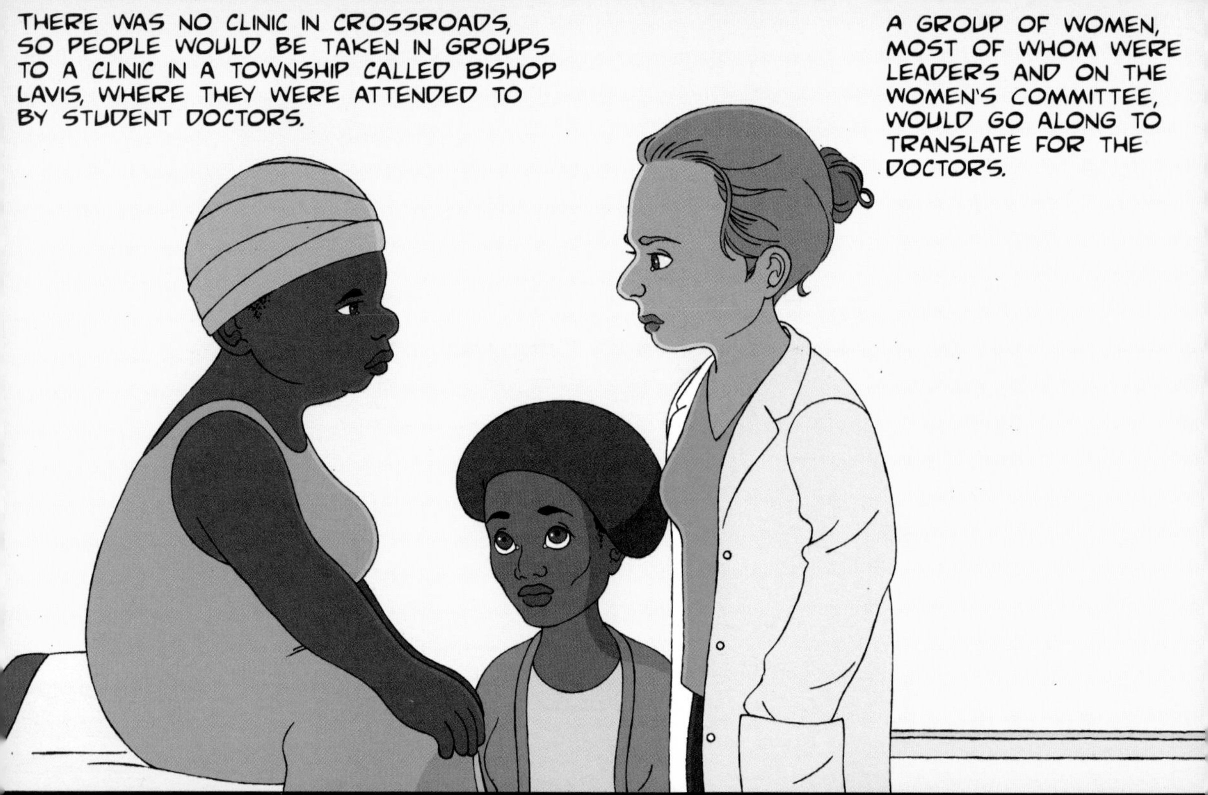
THERE WAS NO CLINIC IN CROSSROADS, SO PEOPLE WOULD BE TAKEN IN GROUPS TO A CLINIC IN A TOWNSHIP CALLED BISHOP LAVIS, WHERE THEY WERE ATTENDED TO BY STUDENT DOCTORS.
A GROUP OF WOMEN, MOST OF WHOM WERE LEADERS AND ON THE WOMEN'S COMMITTEE, WOULD GO ALONG TO TRANSLATE FOR THE DOCTORS.

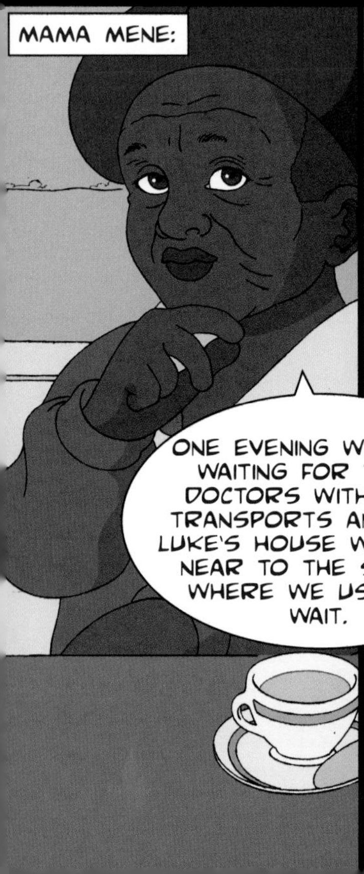
MAMA MENE:
ONE EVENING WE WERE WAITING FOR THESE DOCTORS WITH THEIR TRANSPORTS AND MRS. LUKE'S HOUSE WAS VERY NEAR TO THE SCHOOL WHERE WE USED TO WAIT.

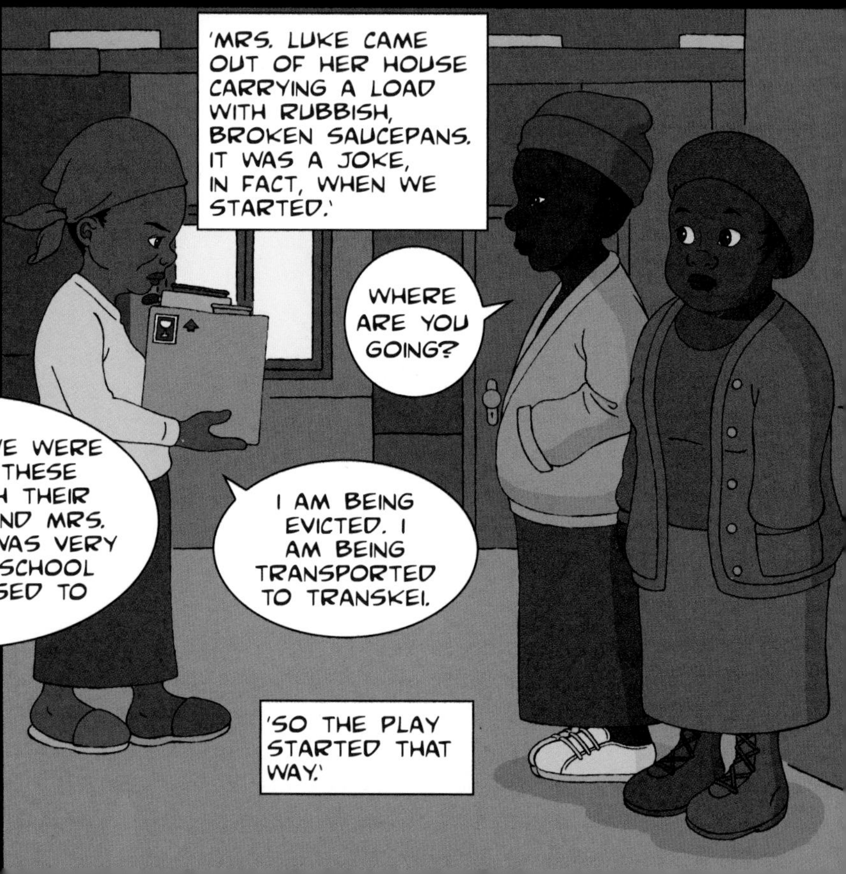
'MRS. LUKE CAME OUT OF HER HOUSE CARRYING A LOAD WITH RUBBISH, BROKEN SAUCEPANS. IT WAS A JOKE, IN FACT, WHEN WE STARTED.'
WHERE ARE YOU GOING?
I AM BEING EVICTED. I AM BEING TRANSPORTED TO TRANSKEI.
'SO THE PLAY STARTED THAT WAY.'

AIDED BY OTHER WOMEN, SQUATTING IN THE CITY AND SUFFERING IN THE BANTUSTANS, SHE CONFRONTS THE POLICE AND AUTHORITIES AND RETURNS TO CAPE TOWN AND LEADS CROSSROADS IN COLLECTIVE RESISTANCE TO A SUCCESSFUL VICTORY TO STAY IN THE CITY.

WHILE THE CORE PLOT WAS STANDARD IN ALL PERFORMANCES, WHAT BROUGHT THE STORY TO LIFE AND CAPTURED THE AUDIENCES WAS THE LAYER OF SYMBOLIC DETAILS IN THE CHARACTERS, THE INTERACTIONS AND THE LINES, WHICH VARIED FROM PERFORMANCE TO PERFORMANCE.

INITIALLY THE CHARACTERS INCLUDED WHITE AND BLACK URBAN POLICE, A COMMUNITY DETERMINED TO STAY, A BLIND WOMAN, A DEPORTED WOMAN, WOMEN IN THE TRANSKEI, AND TRANSKEI POLICEMEN. AS TIME WENT ON, SPECIFIC GOVERNMENT OFFICIALS' WITH WHOM CROSSROADS WAS NEGOTIATING WERE ADDED.

ZUNGOYIKI CROSSROADS, LEMINI IBIKADE IXELWA IFIKILE...

THAT MEANS: DON'T BE AFRAID CROSSROADS — THE DAY WE'VE BEEN WAITING FOR HAS COME.

WHEN WE GET ONTO THE STAGE THAT IS WHAT WE SAY. THE FIRST IMPORTANT THING WAS MUSIC IN THE PLAY BECAUSE IT CONVEYED A MESSAGE.

'IT ASKED QUESTIONS LIKE "SENZENI NA? WHAT HAVE WE DONE? WHY DON'T WE HAVE A PLACE?"'

SET TO THIS MUSIC THE AUDIENCE WATCHED AS WOMEN WALKED ONTO THE STAGE WITH THE MATERIALS THEY USED TO BUILD THEIR SHACKS.

ZUNGOYIKI CROSSROADS, LEMINI IBIKADE IXELWA IFIKILE

'WE WERE CARRYING OUR ZINCS ON THE STAGE — EVERYTHING, LIKE POLES AND ZINCS AND PAPERS. THEN WE STARTED BUILDING OUR HOUSES ON THE STAGE. THEN WE WENT TO BED. THEN I STOOD UP AND SHOUTED BECAUSE I SAW TORCHES, THOSE WERE THE POLICE...'

THE DESCRIPTION AND IMPACT OF RAIDS WERE DRAMATIC, PITTING AFRICAN CHILDREN (PLAYING THE ROLE OF GUARD DOGS) AGAINST STATE ARMORY (POLICE DOGS, ALSO PLAYED BY CHILDREN).

AFTER THE ESTABLISHMENT OF CROSSROADS AND THE IMMEDIATE RAID, TWO WOMEN (PLAYED BY MRS. MGOGO AND MRS. LUKE) ARE ARRESTED.

THE WOMEN APPEAR IN LANGA COURT, ARE FINED APPROXIMATELY R55 FOR NOT HAVING PASSES.

MRS. LUKE IS THEN SERVED NOTICE BY MRS. NTONGANA TO GO STRAIGHT AWAY TO GWATCHU NEAR THE TRANSKEI BORDER WHERE A 'NEW TOWN' IS BEING BUILT, SUPPOSEDLY TO HOUSE PEOPLE FROM CROSSROADS.

BANTU ADMINISTRATION AUTHORITY BOARD OFFICIALS THEN TAKE HER TO HER HOUSE TO FETCH HER BELONGINGS AND FROM THERE SHE IS DRIVEN, IN A POLICE VAN, TO THE TRAIN STATION.

MRS. LUKE AND HER DAUGHTER ARE NEXT SEEN ABOARD A TRAIN. THEY ARRIVE AT BOLOTHWA, THE STATION NEAREST TO GWATCHU.

MRS. LUKE LEAVES HER DAUGHTER NEAR THE STATION WITH THEIR BELONGINGS AND GOES OFF IN SEARCH OF GWATCHU.

SHE LOSES HER WAY AND ARRIVES, WEARY, HUNGRY, AND THIRSTY, AT COFIMVABA IN TRANSKEI.

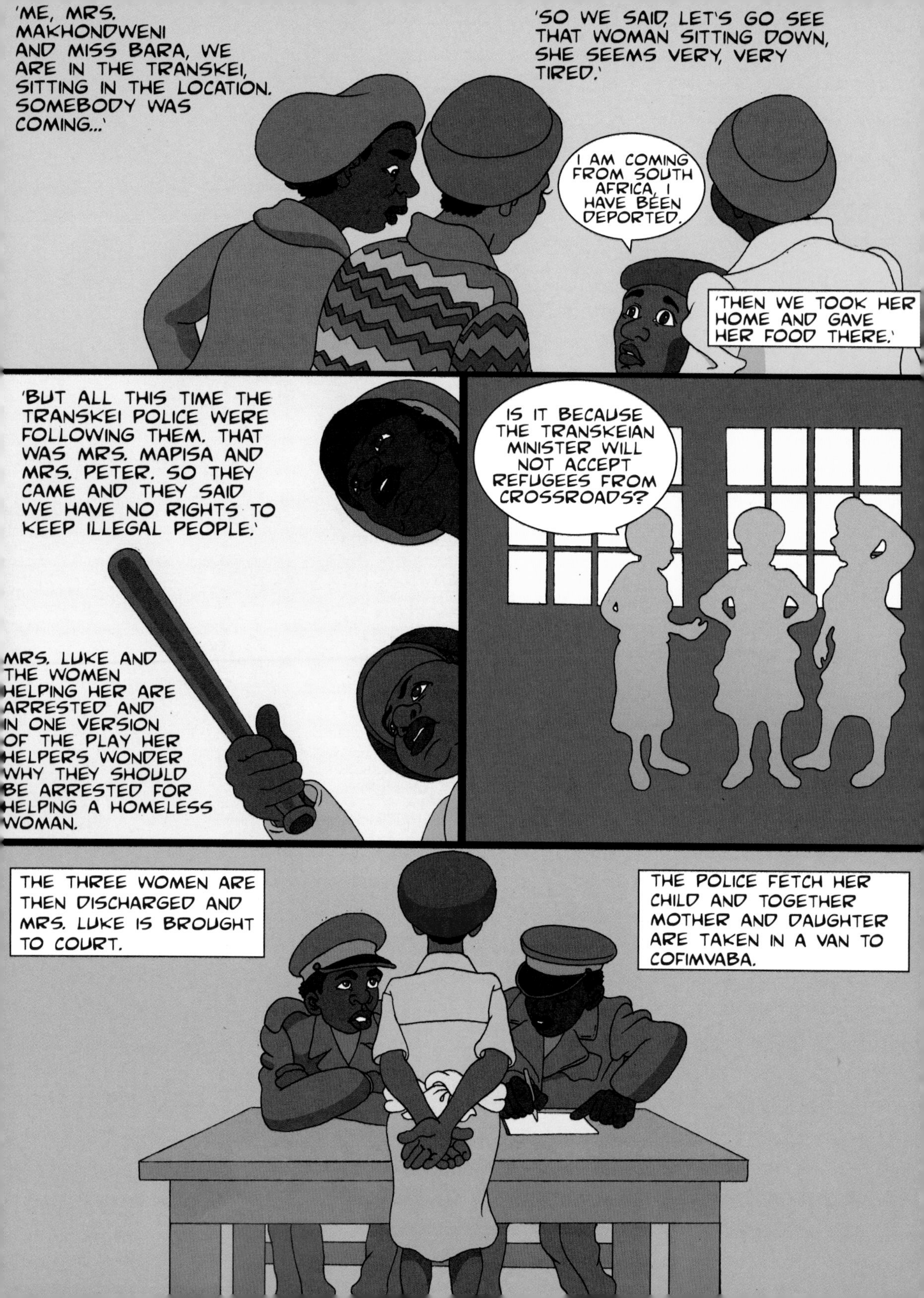
'ME, MRS. MAKHONDWENI AND MISS BARA, WE ARE IN THE TRANSKEI, SITTING IN THE LOCATION. SOMEBODY WAS COMING...'
'SO WE SAID, LET'S GO SEE THAT WOMAN SITTING DOWN, SHE SEEMS VERY, VERY TIRED.'
I AM COMING FROM SOUTH AFRICA, I HAVE BEEN DEPORTED.
'THEN WE TOOK HER HOME AND GAVE HER FOOD THERE.'
'BUT ALL THIS TIME THE TRANSKEI POLICE WERE FOLLOWING THEM. THAT WAS MRS. MAPISA AND MRS. PETER. SO THEY CAME AND THEY SAID WE HAVE NO RIGHTS TO KEEP ILLEGAL PEOPLE.'
MRS. LUKE AND THE WOMEN HELPING HER ARE ARRESTED AND IN ONE VERSION OF THE PLAY HER HELPERS WONDER WHY THEY SHOULD BE ARRESTED FOR HELPING A HOMELESS WOMAN.
IS IT BECAUSE THE TRANSKEIAN MINISTER WILL NOT ACCEPT REFUGEES FROM CROSSROADS?
THE THREE WOMEN ARE THEN DISCHARGED AND MRS. LUKE IS BROUGHT TO COURT.
THE POLICE FETCH HER CHILD AND TOGETHER MOTHER AND DAUGHTER ARE TAKEN IN A VAN TO COFIMVABA.

'WHEN THEY LOCKED HER UP AND SHE WAS IN COURT, SHE TOLD THEM THAT THERE IS NO USE IN ARRESTING HER BECAUSE SHE WILL GO BACK TO CAPE TOWN.'

'AND SHE DID, SHE CAME BACK TO CAPE TOWN.'

AS MRS. LUKE HITCHES HER WAY BACK TO CAPE TOWN, CROSSROADS IS RECEIVING EVICTION NOTICES FROM BAAB AND BEING DEMOLISHED.

THE BULLDOZERS AND FRONT-LOADERS ARRIVE.

HY IS GEMORS MAN. DIE DING IS GEROES. VRRRP-VRRRP!

HA! HA!

HA! HA!

HA! HA!

HOUSES ARE MOWED DOWN AND NEIGHBOURS MOVE AMONGST EACH OTHER IN ANXIETY AND DESPERATION.

IN THE AFTERMATH, WHILE RESIDENTS MOVE ABOUT THE DEVASTATION, SEARCHING OUT THEIR BELONGINGS, MRS. LUKE GOES TO THE SITE OF HER NOW-DESTROYED HOME.

I HAVE COME BACK TO CROSSROADS TO STAY.

THE PLAY ENDS WITH MAMA LUKE PUTTING HER HOUSE BACK UP.

WHAT HAD STARTED SPONTANEOUSLY AS A PLAY PERFORMED FOR AND AMONGST THESE WOMEN, TAKING ON CHARACTERS THEY WERE UP AGAINST AND ACTING OUT THEIR STRUGGLE THUS FAR, QUICKLY EVOLVED INTO SOMETHING MUCH BIGGER.

WITHIN A MONTH THEY HAD CONSOLIDATED THEIR EXPRESSION AND ACCEPTED THE INVITATION OF WHITE ACTIVIST ALLIES TO SUPPORT TAKING THEIR PLAY ON TOUR TO PROJECT THEIR VISION AND DEMANDS IN BANTUSTAN SHACK SETTLEMENTS, LIKE DIMBAZA IN THE CISKEI; IN TOWNSHIPS LIKE SOWETO; AND IN WHITE CITY CENTRES LIKE JOHANNESBURG AND CAPE TOWN.

MAMA MENE:

'WE WERE SO FED UP, MRS. LUKE WAS FED UP. WE WANTED TO PLAY IT (TO EXPOSE IT) — EVEN IN CAPE TOWN PEOPLE DO NOT KNOW HOW WE LIVE.'

'WE WANTED TO SHOW THE OTHER COMMUNITIES, WHITE COMMUNITIES, HOW WE LIVE IN CROSSROADS.'

'SO WE'D BEEN TALKING ABOUT IT AMONGST OURSELVES THAT IT IS HIGH TIME THAT PEOPLE MUST KNOW. EVEN THIS PIK BOTHA THAT GOES OVERSEAS AND TELLS LIES THAT THERE IS PEACE IN SOUTH AFRICA — WE MUST SHOW THE WORLD.'

THIS SMALL IMPROVISATIONAL PLAY PERFORMED ON A PATCH OF DIRT TURNED INTO A THEATRE PIECE ON TOUR TO SOME OF THE BIGGEST PLAYHOUSES IN THE COUNTRY! AFTER A MONTH, WOMEN PERFORMED IT IN CROSSROADS THEN AT THE SPACE THEATRE IN CAPE TOWN. WORD SPREAD AMONGST WHITE LIBERALS AND THE MARKET THEATRE IN JOHANNESBURG CALLED THE VERITAS OFFICE TO REQUEST THE WOMEN COME THERE TO PERFORM.

SEVERAL MONTHS LATER A SECOND TOUR WAS ORGANIZED TO THE EASTERN CAPE WHERE THEY PERFORMED WITH MUCH DRAMA AND SOME TERRIFYINGLY CLOSE CALLS WITH THE POLICE ALONG THE WAY: HOW CAN YOU WOMEN BE TRAVELLING, WITHOUT PASSES, IN A MIXED RACE GROUP, AND WITHOUT HUSBANDS?!

WHITE SUPPORTERS ASSISTED IN THE TOUR IN TERMS OF LOGISTICS BUT HAD NO HAND IN THE CREATION OF THE STORYLINE.

ON NOVEMBER 22, 1978, DR. PIET KOORNHOF SPENT HIS FIRST FULL DAY IN OFFICE VISITING CROSSROADS. TWO DAYS LATER, IMFUDUSO BEGAN ITS RUN AT THE SPACE THEATRE AND WAS WRITTEN UP IN MAJOR NEWSPAPERS IN THE CAPE. AS A REFORMER, KOORNHOF WAS DETERMINED TO CHANGE THE INTERNATIONAL IMAGE OF SOUTH AFRICA BULLDOZING INNOCENT WOMEN'S SHANTIES.

HE USED A LANGUAGE OF MORALITY TO JUSTIFY HIS PROPOSED SOLUTIONS—TAKING A PATERNALISTIC AND PATRONIZING ROLE OF 'GOOD FATHER' AND ARGUING THAT CROSSROADS WAS A 'HEALTH HAZARD' AND NOT A GOOD PLACE TO HAVE 'MEANINGFUL LIVES.'

The Crossroads Question

Required reading: The Riekert Commission Report

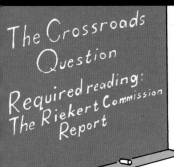

HIS VISIT BEGAN A FOUR-MONTH PERIOD OF INTENSE NEGOTIATIONS WITH THE CROSSROADS COMMITTEES. THE PROCESS WAS BRUTAL.

MAMA YANTA AND MAMA NTONGANA REPRESENTED THE WOMEN'S COMMITTEE ON THE NEGOTIATION TEAM, WHICH WAS ALSO MADE UP OF MALE MEMBERS OF THE JOINT COMMITTEE, ALONG WITH COMMUNITY WORKERS FROM VERITAS LIKE JOSETTE COLE (MANDLOVU) AND CELESTE SANTOS, LAWYER MIKE RICHMAN, UCT PROFESSOR OF ECONOMICS FRANCIS WILSON, AND ANGLICAN BISHOP PATRICK MATALENGWE.

THERE WAS NO CONSENSUS AMONGST THE 'TEAM' ON HOW TO APPROACH NEGOTIATIONS – TO CONTINUE TO EMBARRASS THE STATE OR TO 'COOPERATE' TO ENSURE THE BEST POSSIBLE 'DEAL.'

CROSSROADS MEMBERS OF THE NEGOTIATING TEAM WERE FRUSTRATED BY KOORNHOF'S MANNER AND NEGOTIATION SKILLS. HIS METHODS WERE EXCLUSIONARY AND DIVISIVE: HE WOULD MEET UP WITH THE TEAM AT LARGE ONLY A FEW TIMES AND IN BETWEEN HE WOULD MEET UP WITH THEIR LEGAL TEAM, MADE UP OF RICHMAN AND WILSON, WHO WOULD TAKE PROPOSALS BACK AND FORTH AND ADVISE THE COMMUNITY AT LARGE. WOMEN DECIDED TO CONTINUE PUBLICIZING THEIR MESSAGE THROUGH THE PLAY BUT AGREED TO BE 'ON CALL' FOR KEY MEETINGS. THE FIRST IMFUDUSO PLAY TOOK PLACE IN BETWEEN KOORNHOF NEGOTIATIONS.

JOSETTE COLE

WE WERE UNDER A LOT OF CRITICISMS FOR TAKING THE WOMEN AWAY WHILE THE NEGOTIATIONS WERE GOING ON. WE AGREED IF IT BECOMES CRITICAL WE WOULD SEND THE WOMEN BACK.

AFTER THE PERFORMANCES, INSTEAD OF COMING BACK WITH THE BUS, WE PUT MRS. YANTA AND MRS. NTONGANA ONTO A PLANE AND FLEW THEM FOR THEIR FIRST-EVER PLANE RIDE BACK TO CAPE TOWN. SO IT WAS A PRETTY HECTIC SERIES OF EVENTS.

KOORNHOF ALIENATED AND INTIMIDATED THE DELEGATION FROM THE COMMUNITY.

WALLACE MGOQI

I FELT DEPRESSED. WE WERE LIKE SCHOOL KIDS IN FRONT OF A TEACHER. YOU COULD NOT WHISPER TO YOUR NEIGHBOUR. IT WAS LIKE POLICEMEN WERE WATCHING US...

DR. KOORNHOF TALKED FOR AGES AND AXED THOSE WHO DEEMED TO SAY ANYTHING. WE WERE ALL INTIMIDATED. WE DID NOT GO AS PRAISE SINGERS BUT THAT IS HOW WE TURNED.

WOMEN AND YOUTH RESPONDED DIFFERENTLY.

HOWARD NTLOKO

I AM UNABLE TO TOLERATE THESE MEETINGS. THIS FORM OF DIALOGUE MAKES ONE APPEAR TO BE A SELLOUT. AND THIS I CANNOT TOLERATE. I WOULD LIKE TO CLOSE THE NEGOTIATIONS WITH DR. KOORNHOF TOMORROW, SO THEY CAN GET ON WITH OPPRESSING US, WE CANNOT PARTICIPATE IN A SELLING-OUT PROCESS.

IMFUDUSO FED INTO THE CONFIDENCE OF THE WOMEN, WHO, LIKE THE YOUTH AND UNLIKE THE MEN, DID NOT FLATTER KOORNHOF AT MEETINGS WITH HIM.

NOMANGEZI MBOBOSI

IMFUDUSO WAS VERY POWERFUL. PEOPLE BEGAN TO BECOME STRONG. THE WOMEN'S COMMITTEE NEVER KEPT QUIET. WE CALLED UPON DR. KOORNHOF WHEN WE CAME BACK FROM OUR TOUR. HE GAVE US PROMISES. HE WAS THE MINISTER OF PROMISES.

CAUCUS MEETINGS BETWEEN KOORNHOF AND THE BUSINESS COMMUNITY AND BETWEEN CROSSROADS LEADERS AND THE URBAN FOUNDATION WAS THE BEGINNING OF A PERIOD OF DIVIDE AND RULE THAT WOULD EVENTUALLY PUSH THE WOMEN AND THE KIND OF ORGANIZING THEY EMBODIED OUT OF CROSSROADS.

KOORNHOF DEAL

THE URBAN FOUNDATION'S BIG BUSINESS CONSTITUENTS HAD BEEN KEEN TO DEAL WITH INFLUX CONTROL POLICIES BECAUSE THESE WERE IN THE WAY OF ACCUMULATING CAPITAL. THEY HAD ALREADY MET SECRETLY AT LEAST TWICE SINCE THE SEPTEMBER RAIDS WITH THE CHAIRMEN OF THE SIZAMILE AND NOXOLO COMMITTEES, ELLIOT WAKA AND JOHNSON NGXOBONGWANA.

THE WOMEN'S COMMITTEE WAS TOTALLY UNAWARE OF THESE MEETINGS, ARRANGED WITH THE ASSISTANCE OF BLACK VERITAS COMMUNITY WORKERS.

EXCLUSION WAS NOT INCIDENTAL OR ACCIDENTAL.

JOSETTE COLE: 'UP UNTIL THE KOORNHOF INTERVENTION IT HAD BEEN MEMBERS OF THE WOMEN'S COMMITTEE WHO, TO A LARGE EXTENT, CONTROLLED ACCESS TO INFORMATION, OUTSIDE CONTACTS AND ANY RESOURCES COMING INTO THE COMMUNITY. THE FACT THAT THESE CAUCUS MEETINGS EXCLUDED WOMEN WAS A SIGN THAT CENTRALIZATION MEANT TAKING POLITICAL CONTROL AWAY FROM THEM.'

NEW CROSSROADS

BY LATE MARCH 1979 THE NEGOTIATIONS WERE BREAKING DOWN BECAUSE KOORNHOF WOULD PUT NOTHING IN WRITING THAT GUARANTEED THAT EVERYONE WOULD BE ACCOMMODATED, AND THE COMMUNITY REFUSED TO AGREE TO A SETTLEMENT THAT EXCLUDED ANY CROSSROADS RESIDENTS.

BUT AFTER FOUR MONTHS OF ENDLESS DISCUSSIONS, TIRED, DESPERATE AND WITH NO OTHER ALTERNATIVES BEING OFFERED, THE JOINT COMMITTEE WAS CONVINCED TO 'ACQUIESCE' TO KOORNHOF'S PROPOSAL AND AGREED TO COOPERATE IN BUILDING THE NEW TOWNSHIP.

AT THE END OF THE DAY KOORNHOF HAD MANAGED TO GET THE JOINT COMMITTEE TO AGREE TO A RESETTLEMENT OF CROSSROADS WITH NO GUARANTEE THAT EVERYBODY IN THE COMMUNITY WOULD IN FACT QUALIFY TO LIVE THERE.

FOUR DAYS LATER, BEFORE THE JOINT COMMITTEE HAD EVEN SHARED THIS DECISION WITH THE BROADER COMMUNITY, KOORNHOF PUBLICLY ANNOUNCED HIS SOLUTION TO THE CROSSROADS PROBLEM.

HE TOLD THE PRESS THAT A LARGE NUMBER OF CROSSROADS RESIDENTS WOULD BE MOVED TO A 'NEW CROSSROADS' THAT WOULD BE CONSTRUCTED NEXT DOOR.

JOHNSON

Chapter Four

Witdoeke

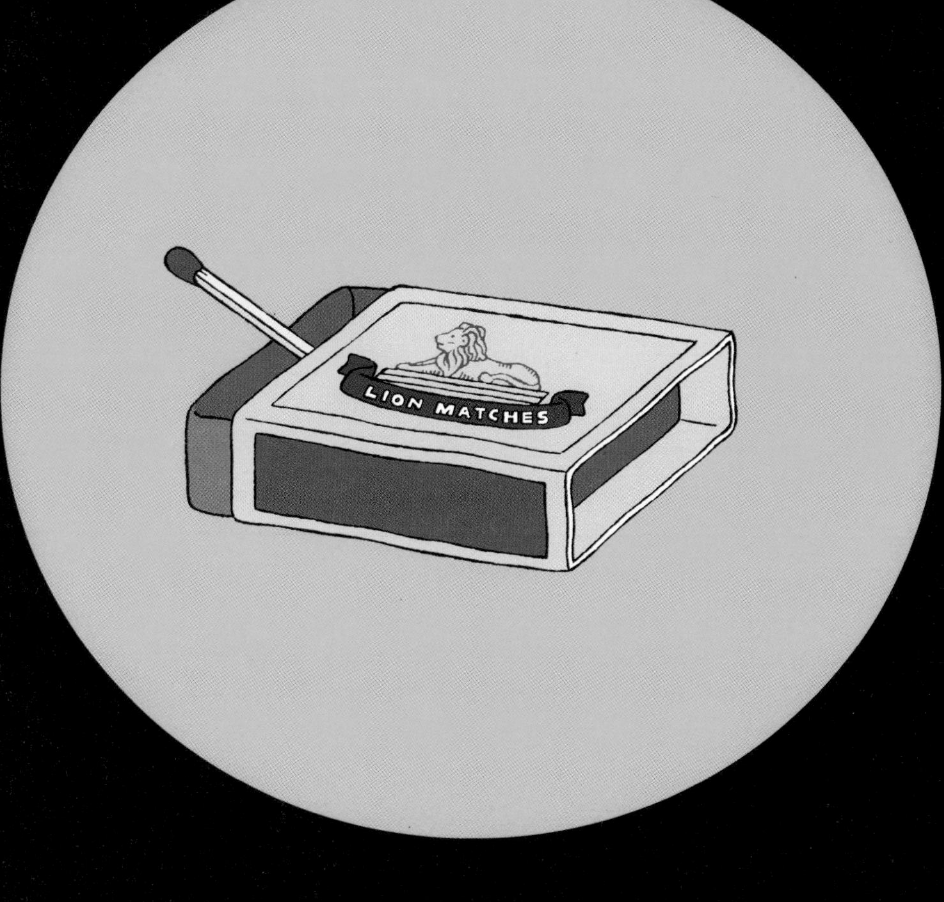
LION MATCHES

IN THE LATE 1970S CROSSROADS WAS KNOWN AS 'A PLACE FULL OF TRANSKEI WOMEN.'

BY THE LATE 1980S IT WAS BEING REFERRED TO AS ICALA LIKITATA, THE 'SIDE' OR 'PLACE OF THE FATHERS.'

THIS TRANSFORMATION WAS NOT INEVITABLE: IT WAS A DIRTY, MULTI-FACETED STRUGGLE.

IT TOOK OVER A DECADE TO RECONFIGURE THE POLITICAL SPACE OF CROSSROADS FROM ONE SYMBOLIZED BY SQUATTER WOMEN'S MOBILIZATION INSPIRING INTERNATIONAL ANTI-APARTHEID RESISTANCE CAMPAIGNS TO ONE OF CORRUPT MILITARIZED CONTROL BY VIGILANTES ARMED AND EMPOWERED BY THE APARTHEID STATE.

THE 1979 NEW DEAL MARKED A TURNING POINT IN THE CROSSROADS STRUGGLE.

IT MARKED A WIN AND A LOSS BOTH AT THE TIME AND IN HINDSIGHT CROSSROADS WOULD NOT BE BULLDOZED, BUT WHO WOULD REMAIN A RESIDENT BECAME A BATTLE, FOUGHT OUT NOT DIRECTLY AGAINST THE STATE BUT WITHIN CROSSROADS ITSELF.

THE KOORNHOF DEAL LAID OUT A RANGE OF CATEGORIES TO LIMIT WHO WOULD QUALIFY FOR HARD-EARNED AND DESPERATELY NEEDED LEGAL AND HOUSING RIGHTS IN THE CITY.

THERE WAS A VAGUE CATEGORY OF AFRICANS WHO WOULD BE OFFERED JOBS AND HOMES IN THE 'HOMELANDS.' 'THIS CONCERNED A SUBSTANTIAL NUMBER OF PARTICULAR CROSSROADS FAMILIES,' SAID THE FINAL AGREEMENT.

KOORNHOF MADE IT CLEAR HE WOULD NOT 'REHOUSE VAGRANTS AND PERSONS OR FAMILIES WITH NO VISIBLE MEANS OF SUPPORT WHICH RENDERED THEM A BURDEN TO THE COMMUNITY ITSELF.'

AS THEY HAD AIMED TO, THE TERMS OF THE 1979 KOORNHOF NEW DEAL RECONFIGURED THE STAGE OF STRUGGLE IN CROSSROADS POLITICS.

THE NEGOTIATIONS AND FINAL DEAL MARKED THE BEGINNING OF THE END OF WOMEN'S INFLUENCE IN CROSSROADS POLITICS.

LIKE LATER NEGOTIATED SETTLEMENTS IN SOUTH AFRICA, CORE PRINCIPLES UNDERLYING THE NEW DEAL STOOD IN OPPOSITION TO THE VISION CROSSROADS WOMEN HAD DRAMATIZED IN IMFUDUSO, THEIR POWERFUL THEATRICAL PRODUCTION ABOUT THEIR STRUGGLE TO SURVIVE AND THRIVE IN CAPE TOWN. AS THE NEW DISPENSATION TOOK HOLD, WOMEN'S ORGANIZING WAS OVERTLY AND COVERTLY STAGNATED, TURNING IMFUDUSO INTO INSPIRATION FROM THE PAST.

CROSSROADS WOMEN HAD BEEN ACKNOWLEDGED FOR THEIR WORK IN GETTING THE STATE TO THE NEGOTIATION TABLE BUT WERE QUICKLY DISMISSED ONCE THEIR STRUGGLE FOR A HOME BECAME A STRUGGLE TO CONTROL ACCESS TO HOUSING.

NOMANGEZI MBOBOSI DESCRIBED THE SITUATION: 'NOW WHEN THE POT WAS NEARLY READY, THE MEN STARTED TO FIGHT.'

IT QUICKLY BECAME IMPOSSIBLE FOR ANYONE TO REMAIN NEUTRAL, INCLUDING THE WOMEN.

WOMEN JOINED THE NEW ALL-MALE EXECUTIVE COMMITTEE IN PRESSURING THE STATE TO INCLUDE PEOPLE FROM CROSSROADS IN THE REQUIRED PROCESS OF SURVEYING CROSSROADS TO DETERMINE WHO WOULD QUALIFY FOR THE PROMISED NEW ACCOMODATION.

20 CROSSROADS RESIDENTS AND 20 BANTU AFFAIRS ADMINISTRATION BOARD OFFICIALS WERE SELECTED TO WORK TOGETHER TO CARRY OUT THIS SURVEY, ONLY AFTER THE CONTROVERSIAL QUESTIONNAIRE WAS DRAFTED AND REDRAFTED IN AN ATTEMPT TO PROTECT AND INCLUDE AS MANY SQUATTERS AGAINST THE BEAST OF APARTHEID BUREAUCRACY THAT AIMED TO CATEGORIZE AND EXCLUDE.

ATTEMPTS TO INFLUENCE THE OUTCOMES OF THE SURVEY BECAME FRAUGHT WITH TENSIONS THAT ULTIMATELY FED INTO A CESSPOOL OF DIVISION AND INDIRECT RULE COMMON TO EXPERIENCES OF COLONIZATION WORLDWIDE.

ONCE BUILT, HOUSES IN NEW CROSSROADS STOOD EMPTY FOR MANY MONTHS.

THERE WERE A NUMBER OF REASONS THAT PEOPLE WERE RELUCTANT TO MOVE: THE BREAKING OF SOCIAL NETWORKS AND COPING MECHANISMS; HIGHER RENTALS; AND INTIMIDATION BY SOME RESIDENTS IN THE SURROUNDING AREAS OF NYANGA AND GUGULETHU WHO ALSO NEEDED HOUSES AND FELT THAT SQUATTERS HAD UNDERMINED THE WAITING LISTS THAT TOWNSHIP RESIDENTS LIVING IN OVERCROWDED HOUSES AND BACKYARD SHACKS HAD BEEN ON FOR YEARS.

THE CROSSROADS 'LISTS' WERE EQUALLY DIVISIVE: ONLY PEOPLE LISTED ON THE 1976 AND 1980 SURVEYS AT CROSSROADS WERE ALLOWED TO MOVE TO NEW CROSSROADS, WHICH EXCLUDED FAMILY MEMBERS AND SUBLETTERS.

TENSIONS ALSO CAME FROM OLD CROSSROADS RESIDENTS WHO DID NOT QUALIFY FOR OR BELIEVE IN THE MOVE.

IN ADDITION, NOT ALL HOUSES IN NEW CROSSROADS WERE GIVEN TO PEOPLE FROM OLD CROSSROADS WHICH CAUSED TENSIONS BETWEEN THOSE WHO GOT THE HOUSES. THIS INCLUDED PEOPLE FROM THE NEARBY KTC SQUATTER CAMP.

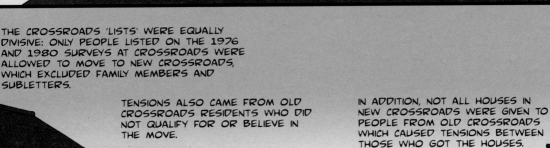

MOVING TO NEW CROSSROADS WAS SEEN BY MANY IMFUDUSO WOMEN AS A MILESTONE IN DIVISION WHERE WOMEN'S ALLIANCES WERE SLOWLY SEVERED.

MAMA MAPISA:

ON OUR ARRIVAL HERE WE STOPPED PERFORMING THAT PLAY, BECAUSE NOW ALL OF US HAVE HOUSES.

THE LEGACY OF THE STRUGGLE IN OLD CROSSROADS FOR THE RIGHT TO LIVE IN THE CITY ENGENDERED A FIERCE DEFENSIVENESS OF THEIR NEW HOMES IN NEW CROSSROADS, ESPECIALLY AMONG THE OLDER WOMEN WHO HAD SUFFERED REPEATED ENDORSEMENT OUT OF THE CITY AND HAD BEEN CONSTANTLY HARASSED BY THE AUTHORITIES.

MAMA LUKE REMAINED IN OLD CROSSROADS. HER DAUGHTER, SIPOKAZI, EXPLAINED WHY:

MY MOM WAS THE ONLY ONE WHO WAS LEFT IN CROSSROADS BY CHOICE.

THE WHOLE CAST OF IMFUDUSO WAS IN NEW CROSSROADS EXCEPT MY MOM...NGXOBONGWANA WAS IN CHARGE AND HE'D SAY IF YOU WANT TO GO TO NEW CROSSROADS YOU HAVE THE RIGHT TO DO SO AND IF YOU DON'T WANT TO GO YOU HAVE THE RIGHT TO DO SO.

94

THERE WERE A LOT OF PEOPLE THAT DID NOT WANT TO GO. SHE HAD HER OWN NETWORKS. I DON'T THINK SHE WANTED TO CUT THOSE TIES. ECONOMICALLY, IT DID NOT MAKE SENSE.

New Crossroads

IN SPITE OF TENSIONS CAUSED BY THE MOVE THERE WAS AN ATTEMPT MADE BY MAMA NTONGANA TO LINK WOMEN FROM OLD AND NEW CROSSROADS, INITIATING NOMZAMO (ISIXHOSA FOR 'SHE WHO STRUGGLES').

HOWEVER, THIS PROVED UNSUSTAINABLE.

Old Crossroads

NOMANGEZI: 'WE TRIED BUT IT DID NOT EXIST BECAUSE THERE WERE TWO SIDES ALL THE TIME. WE NEVER DID EXACTLY WHAT WE DID IN CROSS- ROADS: TO BE ONE BODY. WE WERE DIVIDED IN NEW CROSSROADS. THE SEPERATION RULE OF THE BOERE WORKED OVER THERE.'

HOUSING HAD ALWAYS BEEN A MEANS OF SOCIAL CONTROL AND GOVERNMENT-SPURRED DIVISIONS WAS THE MOST COMMON REASON GIVEN TO EXPLAIN WHY ATTEMPTS TO REORGANIZE A WOMEN'S COMMITTEE IN NEW CROSSROADS FAILED.

McENNA 2015 Feb.

WHILE WOMEN'S ORGANIZING WAS GRADUALLY POLITICALLY MARGINALIZED, THE MESSAGE OF IMFUDUSO CONTINUED TO INSPIRE MORE AND MORE DISPOSSESSED AND EXCLUDED PEOPLE TO COME AND OCCUPY PIECES OF LAND SURROUNDING CROSSROADS.

KOORNHOF ADOPTED A BRUTAL ZERO-TOLERANCE POLICY AFTER THE DEAL, WHICH HE JUSTIFIED AS BEING

...IN THE INTEREST OF THE SQUATTERS THEMSELVES.

THE NYANGA BUSH CAMP RECEIVED NATIONAL ATTENTION WHEN THE STATE TEAR-GASSED PROTESTERS OUTSIDE THE COURTHOUSE WHEN THESE NEW SQUATTERS WERE ARRESTED.

AS FAR AS THE STATE WAS CONCERNED, THE CROSSROADS DEAL HAD TO REMAIN UNIQUE. IF IT BECAME A PRECEDENT THEY WOULD HAVE TO ACCEPT THE END OF INFLUX CONTROL.

DEPORTATIONS TO THE BANTUSTANS BEGAN ANEW, CAUSING A MASSIVE OUTCRY THROUGHOUT THE COUNTRY.

IN MARCH 1982, 56 SQUATTERS FROM NYANGA BUSH WHO HAD TAKEN REFUGE AT ST. GEORGE'S CATHEDRAL IN THE CENTRE OF CAPE TOWN WENT ON HUNGER STRIKE. ONE WOMAN SUFFERED A MISCARRIAGE BUT CONTINUED TO FAST.

AFTER THREE DAYS OF NEGOTIATIONS BETWEEN THE OCCUPIERS AND KOORNHOF, WITH THE COUNCIL OF CHURCHES AS ARBITRATOR, THE 24-DAY FAST ENDED WHEN THE GOVERNMENT AGREED TO DEAL 'COMPASSIONATELY' WITH 350 SQUATTERS.

THE STATE'S RESPONSE TO OCCUPATION WAS INCREASING THE BAD PRESS THE CROSSROADS DEAL HAD TRIED TO REVERSE.

SOCIAL STRUGGLE PROLIFERATED IN THIS PERIOD AS THE STATE ATTEMPTED TO BACKTRACK ON THE PROMISES MADE.

IN OLD CROSSROADS DELAYS FOR PERMITS CONTINUED. RAIDS INTENSIFIED, ROUNDING UP THOSE 'PROMISED' PERMITS AND HOUSES REGARDLESS OF THE ORIGINAL LISTS AND SURVEYS.

APARTHEID STATE REFORMS CREATED 'URBAN INSIDERS' AND 'RURAL OUTSIDERS.' THE GOAL WAS ECONOMIC CO-OPTATION OF THE URBAN INSIDER, WHOSE POSITION WAS IMPROVED AT THE EXPENSE OF THE OUTSIDER.

URBAN INSIDERS, WHO WERE GIVEN THE STATUS OF 'LEGALS,' WERE GIVEN MORE OPPORTUNITY FOR OCCUPATIONAL AND GEOGRAPHIC MOBILITY.

RURAL OUTSIDERS, OR 'ILLEGALS,' WERE TREATED AS FOREIGNERS FROM THE BANTUSTANS AND FACED STRICTER LAWS GOVERNING THEIR URBAN PRESENCE AS TEMPORARY CONTRACT AND SURPLUS LABOUR.

THE QUALITY OF LIFE FOR QUALIFYING URBAN BLACK PEOPLE IMPROVED DRAMATICALLY.

HOWEVER, THEY AND THEIR DEPENDENTS CONSTITUTED ONLY ABOUT ONE AND A HALF MILLION PEOPLE, AS COMPARED TO THE TOTAL BLACK POPULATION OF 20 MILLION FOR SOUTH AFRICA AS A WHOLE.

LIFE FOR OUTSIDERS, AS THE EXAMPLE OF NYANGA BUSH DEMONSTRATED, WOULD BE MADE INFINITELY WORSE.

IN CROSSROADS NGXOBONGWANA INVERTED THE INSIDER-OUTSIDER DIVIDE BY REDEFINING AN INSIDER AS SOMEONE WITH A RIGHT TO CONCESSIONS MADE TO CROSSROADS AS A PLACE FOR THOSE WITHOUT SECTION 10 RIGHTS. THUS AS REMOVALS OF SQUATTERS BY THE STATE CONTINUED, A SECOND KIND OF REMOVAL BEGAN—THOSE CARRIED OUT BY THE NEW CROSS-ROADS LEADERSHIP. THIS INTERNAL RECONFIGURATION OF POLITICAL POWER STRUGGLES SUFFOCATED IMFUDUSO WOMEN'S MESSAGE AND PREVIOUS ABILITY TO MAKE AND DEFEND CROSSROADS AS A PLACE FOR DISPLACED WOMEN.

AS CROSSROADS GREW, THE COMPETITIVE STAKES FOR CONTROLLING PEOPLE AND TERRITORY INCREASED. BY THE END OF 1979 ANY INTERNAL OPPOSITION TO THE NEWLY CONSTRUCTED ALL-MALE EXECUTIVE THAT CONTROLLED ALL ASPECTS OF COMMUNITY LIFE FROM EDUCATION TO THE YOUTH TO THE CRÈCHES, WAS QUICKLY CRUSHED.

THE HOMEGUARDS, A SELF-STYLED, SEMI-MILITARY POLICE UNIT WITHIN CROSSROADS, WAS UNDER THE CONTROL OF ONE OF THE HEADMEN, MR. SAM NDIMA.

FOLLOWING THE NEGOTIATION PROCESS, HEADMEN WHO RULED AT A LOCAL LEVEL WERE NECESSARY ALLIES FOR EFFECTING POLITICAL CONTROL, AS WELL AS ACCUMULATING CAPITAL.

NGXOBONGWANA HAD THE ABILITY TO STRADDLE BOTH GROUPS AND BECOME THE SYMBOL OF A CHIEF.

THOUSANDS OF HOMELESS PEOPLE STREAMING INTO THE AREA DURING THE LATTER HALF OF 1984 FOUND THEMSELVES UNDER THE AUTHORITY OF ABOUT 15 LEADERS.

FROM 1980 ONWARDS PATRONAGE AND PATRIARCHY WERE MIXED INTO BATTLE AGAINST THE STATE.

WHILE WIDELY RESPECTED FOR HIS ABILITY TO CHALLENGE WHITE AUTHORITY, THERE WAS GROWING SKEPTICISM OF NGXOBONGWANA'S GROWING WEALTH.

PEOPLE WERE FRUSTRATED WITH THE 'RENT' THEY HAD TO PAY HIM. DURING HIS IMPRISONMENT (IN EARLY 1981, SUPPOSEDLY FOR SELLING TEMPORARY IDS) OLIVER MEMANI LED A SPLIT IN THE EXECUTIVE.

IN RETALIATION, EIGHT 'MEMANI MEN' WERE MURDERED AND MEMANI'S HOUSE IMMEDIATELY GUTTED.

MEMANI FLED TO KTC WHICH WAS SUBSEQUENTLY SURROUNDED BY NGXOBONGWANA'S 'ARMY': MEN WIELDING PANGAS AND IRON BARS LOOKING FOR MEMANI SUPPORTERS AND WEARING WHITE HEADBANDS TO IDENTIFY THEMSELVES.

THE WHITE SCARVES BECAME KNOWN AS 'WITDOEKE.' THE HEAD-CLOTHS HAD INITIALLY BEEN WORN BY OLDER MIGRANTS DURING CONFLICT IN THE LANGA HOSTELS IN THE PAST AND WOULD COME TO REPRESENT 'OLDER MEN' WITH A MIGRANT BACKGROUND AS OPPOSED TO YOUTH OR CAPE-BORNERS.

WITDOEKE WOULD BE USED AS PRO-NGXOBONGWANA, PRO-CONTROL OF CROSSROADS BY CONSERVATIVE 'XHOSA-TRADITIONAL' MEN AND PRO-PEOPLE WITHOUT RIGHTS. IMPORTANTLY, THEY REPRESENTED PEOPLE WHO FELT THREATENED BY NEWCOMERS.

BY THE END OF 1983, NGXOBONGWANA AND HIS ALLIES HAD COMPLETE CONTROL OVER BOTH OLD AND NEW CROSSROADS.

THIS CONTROL WAS BUILT ON A COMBINATION OF COERCION, CONSENT AND RELATIVE

IN 1983, KOORNHOF ANNOUNCED THAT FUTURE PHASES OF CROSSROADS HOUSING DEVELOPMENT WOULD NOT HAPPEN.

THE ANNOUNCEMENT MET WITH SHARP CRITICISM FROM THE NEWLY FORMED UNITED DEMOCRATIC FRONT (UDF), THE FIRST LEGAL AND NATIONAL MASS POLITICAL ORGANIZATION SINCE THE 1950S.

INSTEAD ALL FUTURE HOUSING DEVELOPMENTS FOR AFRICANS GIVEN PERMITS TO BE IN THE CAPE WOULD HAPPEN ON DESOLATE SAND DUNES 30 KILOMETERS AWAY FROM THE CITY.

ASIYI eKHAYELITSHA

WE DEMAND HOUSES, SECURITY AND COMFORT

THE UDF LAUNCHED A DEFIANCE CAMPAIGN: 'ASIYI EKHAYELITSHA' (WE ARE NOT GOING TO KHAYELITSHA).

THE FIRST PEOPLE SCHEDULED TO BE MOVED TO KHAYELITSHA WERE THE INHABITANTS OF CROSSROADS.

SQUATTERS IN CROSSROADS WERE NOW AS VULNERABLE AS ANY IN THE CAPE AND RAIDS BEGAN ANEW.

THE CROSSROADS EXECUTIVE COMMITTEE INFORMED THE PRESS THAT THE PROPONENTS OF A MOVE TO KHAYELITSHA 'WILL HAVE TO KILL US FIRST AND THEN MOVE OUR BODIES TO KHAYELITSHA, BECAUSE THAT IS THE ONLY WAY WE WILL MOVE THERE.'

AN AVERAGE OF 48 HOMES A DAY WERE DEMOLISHED IN THE CROSSROADS COMPLEX AT THIS TIME.

THE MAJORITY REFUSED TO LEAVE AND CROSSROADS CONTINUED TO GROW. NGXOBONGWANA LED THIS RESISTANCE.

THE SUPPORT OF BOTH THE UDF AND THE WESTERN CAPE CIVIC ASSOCIATION INCREASED NGXOBONGWANA'S SENSE OF POWER AND LEGITIMACY AND CREATED A CONFLICT WITHIN A CONFLICT: AS THE UDF INTENSIFIED ITS ANTI-REMOVAL CAMPAIGN, MORE AND MORE PEOPLE LEFT OLD CROSSROADS IN AN ATTEMPT TO ESCAPE THE INCREASING REPRESSION WITHIN THEIR OWN COMMUNITY.

NGXOBONGWANA'S DOMINATION CREATED SUSPICION AND LOSS OF CREDIBILITY RATHER THAN THE SOLIDARITY NEEDED TO SUCCESSFULLY FIGHT FOR THE CITY.

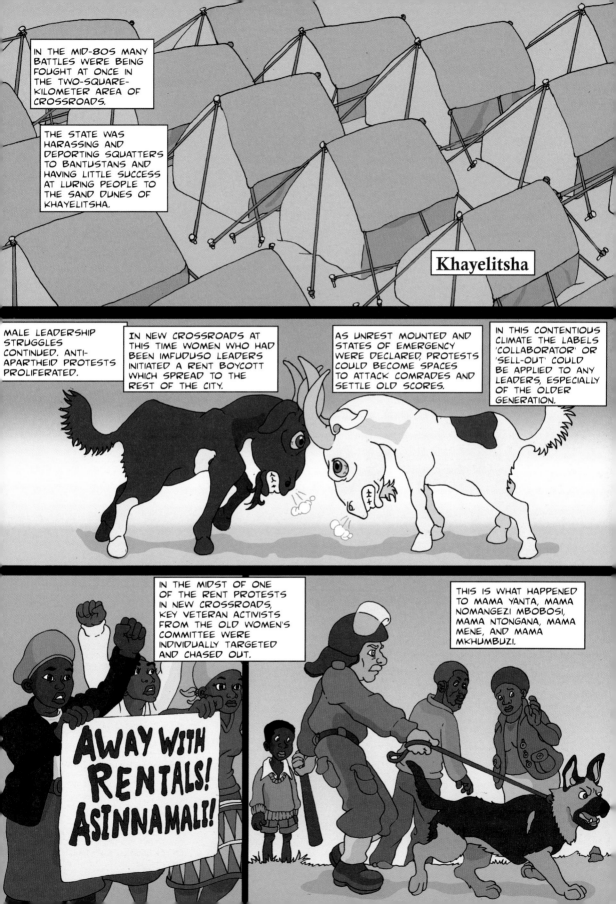

IN THE MID-80S MANY BATTLES WERE BEING FOUGHT AT ONCE IN THE TWO-SQUARE-KILOMETER AREA OF CROSSROADS.

THE STATE WAS HARASSING AND DEPORTING SQUATTERS TO BANTUSTANS AND HAVING LITTLE SUCCESS AT LURING PEOPLE TO THE SAND DUNES OF KHAYELITSHA.

Khayelitsha

MALE LEADERSHIP STRUGGLES CONTINUED. ANTI-APARTHEID PROTESTS PROLIFERATED.

IN NEW CROSSROADS AT THIS TIME WOMEN WHO HAD BEEN IMFUDUSO LEADERS INITIATED A RENT BOYCOTT WHICH SPREAD TO THE REST OF THE CITY.

AS UNREST MOUNTED AND STATES OF EMERGENCY WERE DECLARED, PROTESTS COULD BECOME SPACES TO ATTACK COMRADES AND SETTLE OLD SCORES.

IN THIS CONTENTIOUS CLIMATE THE LABELS 'COLLABORATOR' OR 'SELL-OUT' COULD BE APPLIED TO ANY LEADERS, ESPECIALLY OF THE OLDER GENERATION.

IN THE MIDST OF ONE OF THE RENT PROTESTS IN NEW CROSSROADS, KEY VETERAN ACTIVISTS FROM THE OLD WOMEN'S COMMITTEE WERE INDIVIDUALLY TARGETED AND CHASED OUT.

THIS IS WHAT HAPPENED TO MAMA YANTA, MAMA NOMANGEZI MBOBOSI, MAMA NTONGANA, MAMA MENE, AND MAMA MKHUMBUZI.

AWAY WITH RENTALS! ASINNAMALI!

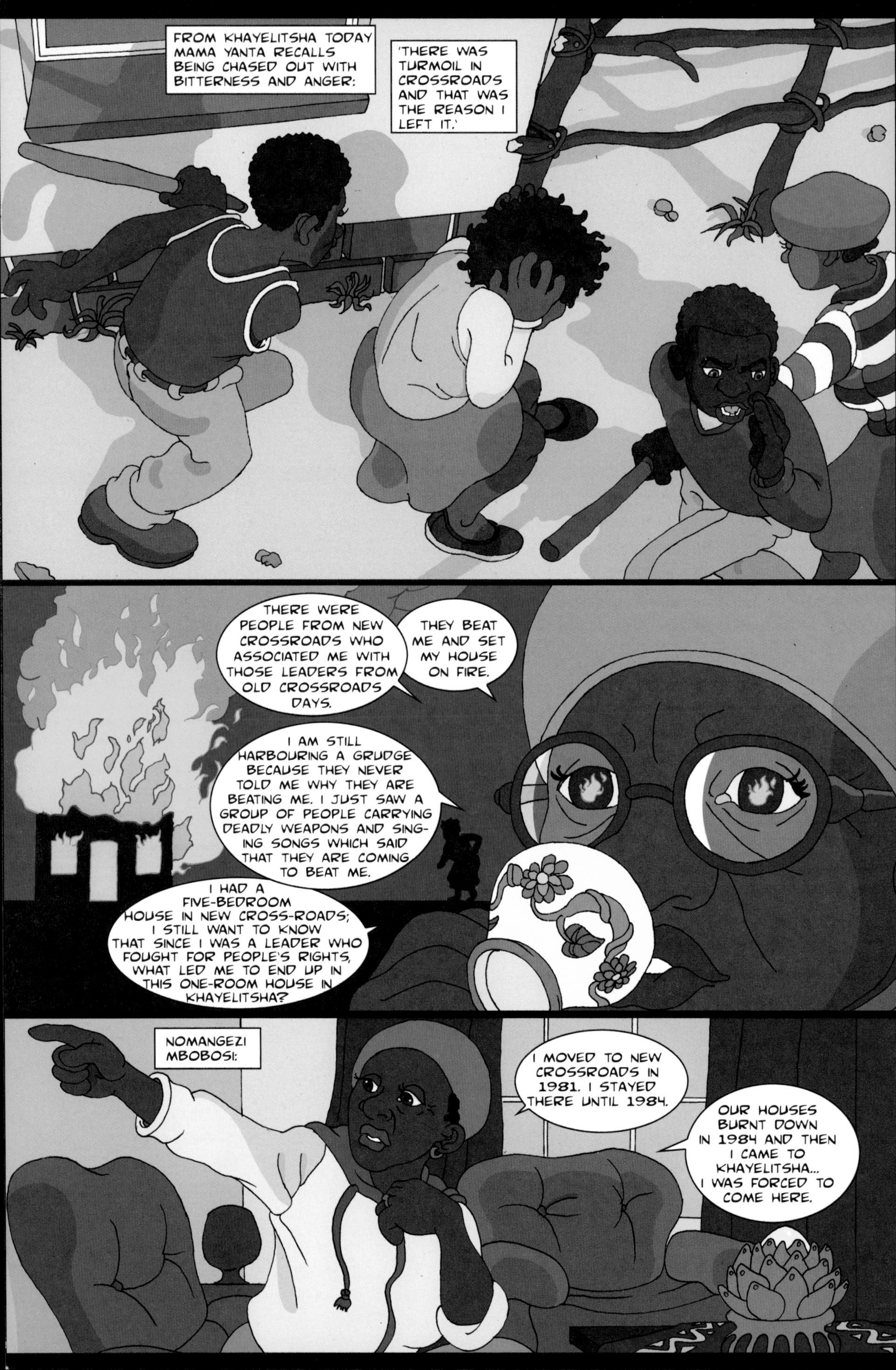

FROM KHAYELITSHA TODAY MAMA YANTA RECALLS BEING CHASED OUT WITH BITTERNESS AND ANGER:
'THERE WAS TURMOIL IN CROSSROADS AND THAT WAS THE REASON I LEFT IT.'
THERE WERE PEOPLE FROM NEW CROSSROADS WHO ASSOCIATED ME WITH THOSE LEADERS FROM OLD CROSSROADS DAYS.
THEY BEAT ME AND SET MY HOUSE ON FIRE.
I AM STILL HARBOURING A GRUDGE BECAUSE THEY NEVER TOLD ME WHY THEY ARE BEATING ME. I JUST SAW A GROUP OF PEOPLE CARRYING DEADLY WEAPONS AND SING-ING SONGS WHICH SAID THAT THEY ARE COMING TO BEAT ME.
I HAD A FIVE-BEDROOM HOUSE IN NEW CROSS-ROADS; I STILL WANT TO KNOW THAT SINCE I WAS A LEADER WHO FOUGHT FOR PEOPLE'S RIGHTS, WHAT LED ME TO END UP IN THIS ONE-ROOM HOUSE IN KHAYELITSHA?
NOMANGEZI MBOBOSI:
I MOVED TO NEW CROSSROADS IN 1981. I STAYED THERE UNTIL 1984.
OUR HOUSES BURNT DOWN IN 1984 AND THEN I CAME TO KHAYELITSHA... I WAS FORCED TO COME HERE.

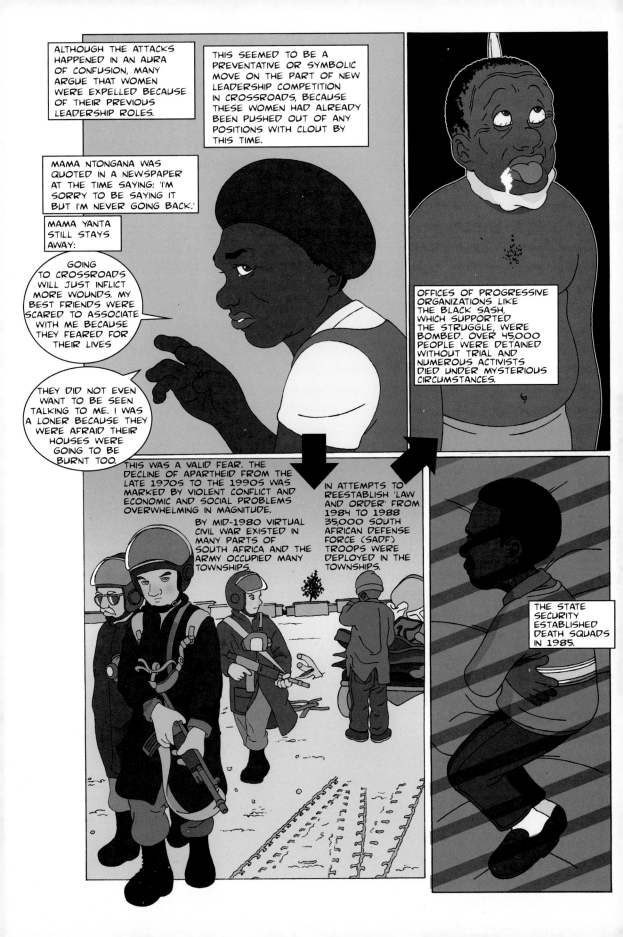

ALTHOUGH THE ATTACKS HAPPENED IN AN AURA OF CONFUSION, MANY ARGUE THAT WOMEN WERE EXPELLED BECAUSE OF THEIR PREVIOUS LEADERSHIP ROLES.

THIS SEEMED TO BE A PREVENTATIVE OR SYMBOLIC MOVE ON THE PART OF NEW LEADERSHIP COMPETITION IN CROSSROADS, BECAUSE THESE WOMEN HAD ALREADY BEEN PUSHED OUT OF ANY POSITIONS WITH CLOUT BY THIS TIME.

MAMA NTONGANA WAS QUOTED IN A NEWSPAPER AT THE TIME SAYING: 'I'M SORRY TO BE SAYING IT BUT I'M NEVER GOING BACK.'

MAMA YANTA STILL STAYS AWAY:

GOING TO CROSSROADS WILL JUST INFLICT MORE WOUNDS. MY BEST FRIENDS WERE SCARED TO ASSOCIATE WITH ME BECAUSE THEY FEARED FOR THEIR LIVES

THEY DID NOT EVEN WANT TO BE SEEN TALKING TO ME. I WAS A LONER BECAUSE THEY WERE AFRAID THEIR HOUSES WERE GOING TO BE BURNT TOO.

OFFICES OF PROGRESSIVE ORGANIZATIONS LIKE THE BLACK SASH, WHICH SUPPORTED THE STRUGGLE, WERE BOMBED. OVER 45,000 PEOPLE WERE DETAINED WITHOUT TRIAL AND NUMEROUS ACTIVISTS DIED UNDER MYSTERIOUS CIRCUMSTANCES.

THIS WAS A VALID FEAR. THE DECLINE OF APARTHEID FROM THE LATE 1970S TO THE 1990S WAS MARKED BY VIOLENT CONFLICT AND ECONOMIC AND SOCIAL PROBLEMS OVERWHELMING IN MAGNITUDE.

BY MID-1980 VIRTUAL CIVIL WAR EXISTED IN MANY PARTS OF SOUTH AFRICA AND THE ARMY OCCUPIED MANY TOWNSHIPS.

IN ATTEMPTS TO REESTABLISH 'LAW AND ORDER' FROM 1984 TO 1988 35,000 SOUTH AFRICAN DEFENSE FORCE (SADF) TROOPS WERE DEPLOYED IN THE TOWNSHIPS.

THE STATE SECURITY ESTABLISHED DEATH SQUADS IN 1985.

WHAT BECAME DETRIMENTAL TO PEOPLE IN
CROSSROADS WERE THE COUNTER-INSURGENCY
GUERILLA WARFARE TACTICS DEVELOPED IN ALGERIA
AND MODIFIED IN VIETNAM AND COLOMBIA THAT
HAD BEEN ADOPTED BY THE APARTHEID STATE TO
IMPOSE ITS VISION OF REFORM.

THE AIM OF THESE TACTICS WAS TO RIP APART
THE SOCIAL FABRIC OF REBELLIOUS COMMUNITIES
DEEMED 'BLACK SPOTS' BY THE APARTHEID
GOVERNMENT.

MCCUEN'S LOW INTENSITY CONFLICT
THEORY KNOWN AS L.I.C. HAD BEEN
PRESCRIBED IN A 75-PAGE DOCUMENT
ENTITLED 'THE ART OF COUNTER-
REVOLUTIONARY WARFARE' AND
DISTRIBUTED THROUGHOUT THE
MANAGEMENT SECURITY SYSTEM.

COUNTER-REVOLUTIONARY WARFARE
STRATEGY AT THE TIME ASSERTED:

A GOVERNING POWER CAN DEFEAT
ANY REVOLUTIONARY MOVEMENT IF IT
ADOPTS THE REVOLUTIONARY STRATEGY
AND PRINCIPLES AND APPLIES THEM IN
REVERSE. THE PURPOSE IS TO DEFEAT
THE REVOLUTIONARIES WITH THEIR OWN
WEAPONS IN THEIR OWN BATTLEFIELDS.

The Art of
Counter-revolutionary
Warfare

Col. J.J. McCuen

L.I.C. PURPOSEFULLY 'PENETRATES INTO
HOMES, FAMILIES, THE ENTIRE FABRIC OF
GRASSROOTS SOCIAL RELATIONS.'

INFORMAL SETTLEMENTS WERE
ESPECIALLY TARGETED.

IN L.I.C. THERE ARE NO 'CIVILIANS' ...IT
IS A SCIENCE OF WARFARE WHOSE
GOAL OF CONTROLLING THE QUALITATIVE
ASPECTS OF HUMAN LIFE MERITS THE
TERM 'TOTALITARIAN.'

THE STATE WANTED TO LOWER THE DENSITY OF CROSSROADS AND INCREASE ITS ACCESS TO THE AREA IN ORDER TO CRUSH PROGRESSIVE AND YOUTH ORGANIZING.

AT THIS TIME GREATER CROSSROADS, ESPECIALLY KTC, WAS SEEN AS A HUB FOR UMKHONTO WE SIZWE, THE UNDERGROUND ANC MILITARY UNITS KNOWN AS MK COMRADES.

SECURITY FORCES IN THE STATE WERE LOOKING FOR CRACKS TO EXPLOIT.

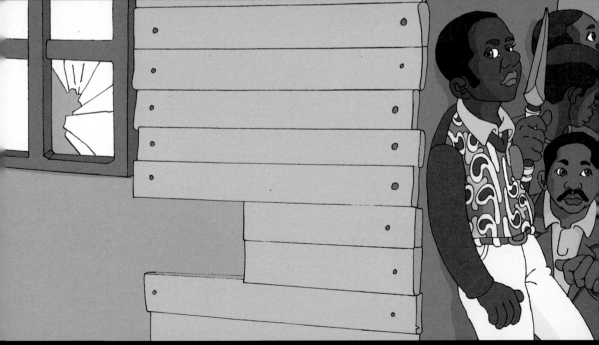

AS THE MOST POWERFUL OF THE LEADERS, NGXOBONGWANA WAS SAID TO HAVE HAD CONTROL OVER 100,000 PEOPLE OUT OF AN ESTIMATED POPULATION OF 150,000 PEOPLE IN CROSSROADS. HOZA, YAMILE, AND TUTU WERE THE MOST IMPORTANT OF THE OTHER LEADERS WHO WERE SAID TO HAVE BETWEEN 40,000 AND 50,000 SUPPORTERS BETWEEN THEM. IT WAS IN THE TERRITORIES OF THESE SMALL LEADERS WHERE THE PROGRESSIVES RECRUITED.

ELESE DEPOUTCH, APPOINTED CROSSROADS WARD COUNCILLOR IN 1996, RECALLS THAT NGXOBONGWANA BANNED THE CAPE YOUTH CONGRESS PERMANENTLY FROM CROSSROADS AND MOST YOUTH FLED TO THE SATELLITE CAMPS OF PORTLAND CEMENT, NYANGA BUSH, AND NYANGA EXTENSION. THESE NEIGHBOURING CAMPS, HE SAID, WERE CONTROLLED BY THREE FORMER HEADMEN WHO HAD REVOLTED AGAINST NGXOBONGWANA'S AUTOCRATIC RULE: 'NGXOBONGWANA THREATENED TO ATTACK THESE CAMPS IF THEY CONTINUED HARBOURING AMAQABANE (COMRADES). HE VOWED TO DEFEND HIS ROLE AS MAYOR OF CROSSROADS AND GET RID OF THE AMAQABANE.' THE EMERGENCE OF VIGILANTES TO PROTECT BLACK TOWNSHIP COUNCILLORS AT THIS TIME

WOMEN'S LEADERSHIP, THE YOUTH TAKING TO THE STREETS OR GOING UNDERGROUND TO JOIN THE ANC WAS SEEN AS A THREAT TO NGXOBONGWANA. THE GROWING POLARIZATION OF 'US' AND 'THEM' MEANT THAT NGXOBONGWANA'S ENEMIES WERE ASSUMED TO BE 'COMRADES' AND ANTI-GOVERNMENT AFFILIATES.

NGXOBONGWANA WAS VULNERABLE AT THIS TIME. HIS SUPPORT WAS DWINDLING. HE HAD BEEN INCARCERATED FOR AN OLD CHARGE RELATED TO THE SELLING OF IDENTITY CARDS AND CORRUPTION OF HOUSING LISTS THAT DATED BACK TO THE DAYS OF THE 1979 SURVEY. AS HIS AUTOCRATIC AND EXCLUSIONARY PRACTICES INTENSIFIED HE BEGAN TO LOSE LEGITIMACY IN CROSSROADS.

YOUTH TOOK THIS OPPORTUNITY TO WIN OVER A NUMBER OF HEADMEN, QUESTIONING NGXOBONG-WANA'S ACCUMULATION OF WEALTH AND ARGUING THAT THE EXECUTIVE SHOULD BE PUSHING FOR CONFRONTATION, NOT NEGOTIATION.

SUPPORTED BY TWO UDF AFFILIATES — THE WESTERN CAPE UNITED WOMEN'S ORGANIZATION AND THE CAPE YOUTH CONGRESS — THEY CONVINCED A NUMBER OF HEADMEN TO FREEZE NGXOBONGWANA'S SALARY (PEGGED BETWEEN 900 TO 4,000 RAND PER MONTH).

IT WAS DURING THIS TIME IN POLLSMOOR PRISON THAT THE STORY OF NGXOBONGWANA TAKES A DRAMATIC TURN, FROM HIS POSITIONING AS COMMUNITY LEADER TO ALIGNING HIMSELF WITH THE BLACK MANAGEMENT COMMITTEE OF APARTHEID LOCAL GOVERNMENT.

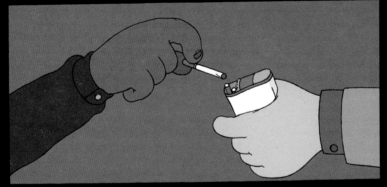

DURING HIS INCARACERATION NGXOBONGWANA WAS VISITED BY THE AUTHORITIES, WHO USED SQUATTERS' THREAT TO HIS POWER AS AN OPPORTUNITY TO RECRUIT HIM AND HIS HEADMEN TO CRUSH PROGRESSIVE FORCES WHO WERE SUCCEEDING IN 'MAKING THE TOWNSHIPS UNGOVERNABLE.'

THEY COULD CONCEIVABLY HAVE OFFERED HIM THE OPTION OF COOPERATION OR KHAYELITSHA.

THEY STRESSED THAT HE WAS ON THE VERGE OF BEING OVER-RUN BY NEW YOUTH ORGANIZATIONS AND BY HIS HEADMEN RIVALS.

NGXOBONGWANA SWITCHED LAWYERS, BROKE WITH THE UDF, AND ONLY GRANTED CERTAIN HEADMEN VISITATION RIGHTS.

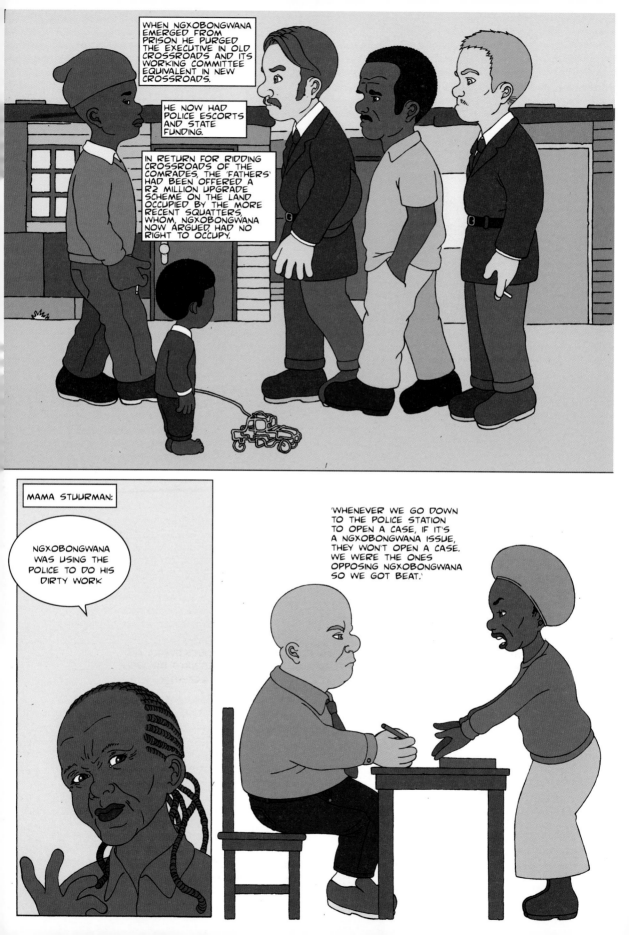

WHEN NGXOBONGWANA EMERGED FROM PRISON HE PURGED THE EXECUTIVE IN OLD CROSSROADS AND ITS WORKING COMMITTEE EQUIVALENT IN NEW CROSSROADS.

HE NOW HAD POLICE ESCORTS AND STATE FUNDING.

IN RETURN FOR RIDDING CROSSROADS OF THE COMRADES, THE 'FATHERS' HAD BEEN OFFERED A R2 MILLION UPGRADE SCHEME ON THE LAND OCCUPIED BY THE MORE RECENT SQUATTERS, WHOM, NGXOBONGWANA NOW ARGUED, HAD NO RIGHT TO OCCUPY.

MAMA STUURMAN:

NGXOBONGWANA WAS USING THE POLICE TO DO HIS DIRTY WORK

'WHENEVER WE GO DOWN TO THE POLICE STATION TO OPEN A CASE, IF IT'S A NGXOBONGWANA ISSUE, THEY WON'T OPEN A CASE. WE WERE THE ONES OPPOSING NGXOBONGWANA SO WE GOT BEAT.'

INTIMIDATION AND FEAR WERE MOUNTING AND WHEN NGXOBONGWANA ORGANIZED A
VOTE TO CONTROL THE UPGRADE, HE FOUND NO WILLING OPPOSITION. BUT HIS OWN
POSITION WAS FAR FROM SECURE.

WHAT FOLLOWED WAS A WELL-DOCUMENTED 30-DAY WAR BETWEEN THE STATE-
SUPPORTED WITDOEKE AND THE PEOPLE OF CROSSROADS, ESPECIALLY THOSE SEEN
TO BE THE ANTI-APARTHEID 'COMRADES.' POLICE ASSISTED NGXOBONGWANA, DRIVING
OUT THOSE WHO WERE SEEN AS A THREAT TO HIS LEADERSHIP AS WELL AS THEIR
'FOLLOWERS' (OR THOSE UNLUCKY ENOUGH TO LIVE IN THEIR 'SECTION') TO THE SAND
DUNES OF KHAYELITSHA.

WITDOEKE WERE THE FOOT SOLDIERS RECRUITED BY NGXOBONGWANA AND
HIS ALLIES, MOSTLY FROM CROSSROADS, BUT INCLUDED RECRUITS BROUGHT
TO CROSSROADS FROM KHAYELITSHA BY HOZA WHO HAD RECENTLY
RELOCATED THERE IN EXCHANGE FOR PERMITS FOR 'HIS PEOPLE.'

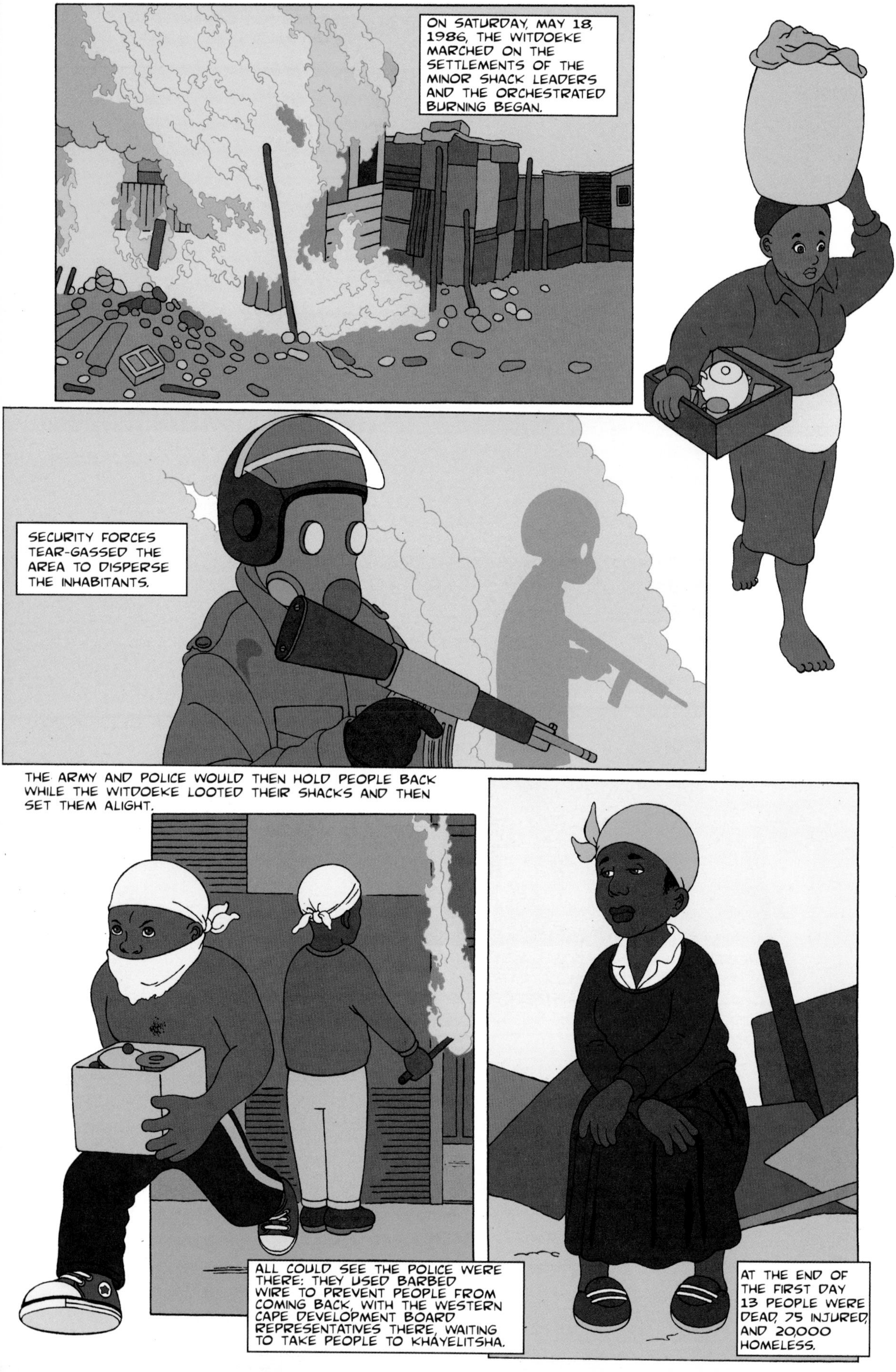
ON SATURDAY, MAY 18, 1986, THE WITDOEKE MARCHED ON THE SETTLEMENTS OF THE MINOR SHACK LEADERS AND THE ORCHESTRATED BURNING BEGAN.
SECURITY FORCES TEAR-GASSED THE AREA TO DISPERSE THE INHABITANTS.
THE ARMY AND POLICE WOULD THEN HOLD PEOPLE BACK WHILE THE WITDOEKE LOOTED THEIR SHACKS AND THEN SET THEM ALIGHT.
ALL COULD SEE THE POLICE WERE THERE: THEY USED BARBED WIRE TO PREVENT PEOPLE FROM COMING BACK, WITH THE WESTERN CAPE DEVELOPMENT BOARD REPRESENTATIVES THERE, WAITING TO TAKE PEOPLE TO KHAYELITSHA.
AT THE END OF THE FIRST DAY 13 PEOPLE WERE DEAD, 75 INJURED, AND 20,000 HOMELESS.

AS A YOUTH WINNIE NKOSI HAD BEEN INVOLVED IN RESISTING FORCED REMOVALS IN OLD CROSSROADS IN THE 1970S.
WE'VE BEEN IN MODDERDAM AND BUILT SHACKS THERE, ELSIES RIVER, WHERE WE PLAYED COLOURED. THEN I WAS 'WINNIE KING' ON MY COLOURED ID, IN WERKGENOT ROAD.
MY HOUSE WAS THE FOURTH HOUSE IN CROSSROADS. I HAD A HOUSE IN RETREAT AND I LEFT IT FOR CROSSROADS. PEOPLE, WHITE PEOPLE, WERE SAYING COME TO CROSSROADS. ONE, TWO, MY AUNTIE AND FOUR – MINE. THEN THE REST CAME.
WE WOULD BUILD HOUSES AT NIGHT...I WAS SO YOUNG AT THE TIME, I DIDN'T EVEN HAVE A CHILD. POLICE WOULD BURN SHACKS AND JAIL US AND WE WOULD RUN AWAY. ALL OF THESE THINGS HAPPENING TO US MADE US KNOW ABOUT ORGANIZATION.
I CALL IT AN ORGANIZATION BECAUSE WE WERE A GROUP – WE DIDN'T KNOW THE ANC YET.

I WORKED UNDERGROUND AND I RAN TO AVOID PRISON. PEOPLE COULD COUNT ON ME. I WAS FULLY SPIRITED.

ONE TIME I DID 90 DAYS IN DETENTION IN THE JAIL ON ROELAND STREET. IN JAIL THERE WERE MANY PEOPLE THERE FOR BREAKING THE LAW. MOSTLY WOMEN IN JAIL. I WAS JAILED WITH MY BABY.

IN 1982 SHE WAS GIVEN A HOUSE IN NEW CROSSROADS AND WAS THEN INVOLVED IN THE RENT BOYCOTTS AND JAILED, THIS TIME IN MITCHELL'S PLAIN.

IN JANUARY 1986 SHE WAS ATTACKED BY WITDOEKE. AT THIS TIME SHE WAS CHAIRWOMAN OF THE UNITED WOMEN'S ORGANIZATION.

NGXOBONGWANA'S ERSTWHILE ENFORCER, SAM NDIMA, SAID THEY PUNISHED HER BECAUSE SHE HAD PASSED ON INFORMATION FROM THEIR MEETINGS.

BUT RECALL HOW, TOGETHER WITH THE YOUTH, THESE RENT BOYCOTTING AND UWO WOMEN HAD PUSHED THE QUESTION OF NGXOBONGWANA'S POWER WHEN HE WAS IN JAIL THE PREVIOUS YEAR.

'WITDOEKE WERE LOOKING FOR ME. ALL THESE MEN WERE LOOKING FOR ONE WOMAN: ME. THEY WANTED ME BECAUSE I HAVE COME WITH POLITICS. NOW THE MEN AND THE WIVES DON'T GET TOGETHER 'COS THE WOMEN ALL COME WITH ME. THE MEN DON'T FEEL WHAT WE FEEL. I WAS SITTING HERE IN THIS HOUSE, WITH A BLACK CUP OF TEA. ALL THESE MEN CAME AND TOOK ME AWAY AND LOCKED ME IN A CONTAINER. WITHOUT A PLACE TO WEE, PASS WATER, NUMBER TWO.'

'IT WAS TWO METERS BY ONE METER. I HAD TO STAND FOR FOUR DAYS. I WET MYSELF.'

'PEOPLE STARTED RIOT-ING TO THE WITDOEKE: WE WANT THAT WOMAN BACK, WE WANT MAMA NKOSI BACK. SHE'S DONE NO WRONG!'

'AFTER FOUR DAYS I WAS BROUGHT BACK. MY HOUSE WAS EMPTY. NO CURTAINS, CARPETS, NOTHING. AND THEN I WANTED NOTHING TO DO WITH STRUGGLE ANYMORE.'

ON JUNE 9 HOZA JOINED NGXOBONGWANA AND THEY MARCHED ON
KTC, DESTROYING MOST OF THE CAMP. 53 PEOPLE WERE KILLED AND
7000 SHACKS DEMOLISHED. SQUATTERS WERE SCATTERED ACROSS
THE CITY, A LARGE NUMBER EVENTUALLY FINDING THEIR WAY TO
KHAYELITSHA, IN SPITE OF ALL THEIR PREVIOUS RESISTANCE.

A FORMER SECURITY BRANCH MEMBER TOLD
THE TRC: 'I FLEW OVER THE SQUATTER CAMP
TO VIEW THE WORK OF THE WITDOEKE...
THEY WERE ATTACKING THE INHABITANTS AND
BURNING THEIR SHACKS. IT LOOKED LIKE A
SUCCESSFUL WAR MISSION, BECAUSE OF THE
'LINE' OF ADVANCE AND THE ENORMITY OF
THE DAMAGE.'

THE ROLE OF POLICE IN CASSPIRS, WEARING
BALACLAVAS, WAS CAPTURED BY THE PRESS.
THE BBC TELEVISED SCENES FROM THE
FRONTLINE AND USED WHITE DOTS TO POINT
OUT THE SOUTH AFRICAN POLICE. YET THE
GOVERNMENT DENIED ANY RESPONSIBILITY
FOR THE TRAGEDY, EXPLAINING THE MAYHEM
AS 'BLACK-ON-BLACK' VIOLENCE.

THE VIGILANTES HAD ACCOMPLISHED IN A FEW WEEKS WHAT THE STATE HAD
FAILED TO DO IN TEN YEARS AND BY SEPTEMBER 126,000 HAD MOVED TO
KHAYELITSHA, WHERE WITDOEKE CONTINUED TO HARASS 'COMRADES.' AT THE
END OF THE 27-DAY WAR AN ESTIMATED 100 PEOPLE WERE DEAD AND
70,000 WERE TURNED INTO
REFUGEES IN THE LAND
OF THEIR BIRTH.

ON JUNE 21, 1986, AFTER INTENSIVE DISCUSSIONS WITH 50-60 OF THE CROSSROADS LEADERS, BISHOP TUTU GOT EACH SIDE TO AGREE TO A CEASEFIRE, REPORTING THAT LEADERS AGREED THAT THEY ARE NOT 'IN THE BUSINESS OF FIGHTING FELLOW BLACKS AND THAT THEY UNDERSTAND THAT THERE IS A MANIPULATION OF A VERY TENSE SITUATION BY CERTAIN INTERESTED PARTIES.'

THE STATE THREW A VICTORY FEAST OF FRESHLY SLAUGHTERED BRAAI MEAT FOR THE WITDOEKE: THE 1996 TRUTH AND RECONCILIATION COMMISSION REVEALED THAT THE R3,000 BUDGET FOR THE PARTY HAD BEEN PRE-APPROVED EVEN BEFORE THE ATTACKS TOOK PLACE.

THE STATE COULD NOW ABOLISH ITS MUCH-CRITICIZED INFLUX CONTROL POLICY IN 1986, HAVING EVACUATED MOST OF THE 100,000 'ILLEGALS' THEY ESTIMATED WERE IN THE CAPE.

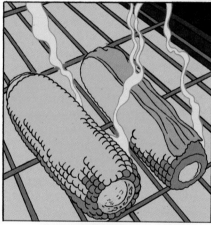

WITDOEKE ROLLED BACK THE SPACES AND GAINS MADE BY WOMEN IN CROSSROADS IN AT LEAST FOUR IMPORTANT WAYS:

FIRST, WITDOEKE WAS A VIOLENT BATTLEFIELD OF MEN WHICH, LIKE OTHER CONFLICT SITUATIONS HAVE SHOWN, ENFORCES A SPECIFIC KIND OF MILITARIZED MASCULINITY ON MEN AND RE-CASTS WOMEN INTO POSITIONS OF INDEPENDENCE AND INFERIORITY.

SECOND, WITDOEKE BURNED DOWN SHACKS AS WELL AS FOUNDATIONAL IDEAS WOMEN HAD HIGHLIGHTED IN THEIR CAMPAIGN THAT CROSSROADS BE A PLACE FOR 'PEOPLE WITHOUT A PLACE.' WITDOEKE IMPOSED THE STATE'S 'ORDERLY (EXCLUSIVE) URBANIZATION' PROGRAM AND MILITARIZED HOUSING ALLOCATION POLITICS. THE FORCED REMOVAL CHASED OUT PEOPLE AND PUT THE ISSUES OF UTMOST IMPORTANCE TO SQUATTER WOMEN ON THE BACKBURNER.

THIRD, THE NEWLY REFORMED URBAN SPACE WOULD BE RUN BY A LOCAL GOVERNMENT OF 'FATHERS,' WHICH MEANT THAT WITDOEKE REASSERTED AND INSTITUTIONALIZED A PARTICULAR VERSION OF TRADITIONAL PATRIARCHY. 'FATHERS' FROZE THE MOST HIERARCHICAL AND SEXIST ASPECTS OF ANYTHING THAT FAINTLY ECHOED ANY PRE-COLONIAL OR RURAL XHOSA 'TRADITION.'

FOURTH, WITDOEKE BROKE CROSS-RACIAL PROGRESSIVE ALLIANCES THAT HAD PREVIOUSLY BEEN BUILT BY WOMEN IN LEADERSHIP AND REDREW THE POLITICAL BOUNDARIES OF THE CROSSROADS STRUGGLE TO BE ONE OF FATHERS VERSUS COMRADES. WOMEN WHO HAD FOUGHT FOR CROSSROADS FIT NEITHER OF THESE OFFICIAL CATEGORIES OF PLAYERS. THIS HAS RESULTED IN THEIR DISAPPEARANCE FROM THIS PHASE OF CROSSROADS HISTORY.

Chapter Five

The Mothers of Crossroads

THE SERIES OF ATTACKS ON OLD CROSSROADS, IN MAY 1986, BY STATE-BACKED WITDOEKE VIGILANTES LEFT MANY DEAD, MANY HOMES BURNT DOWN, AND 70,000 PEOPLE DISPLACED.

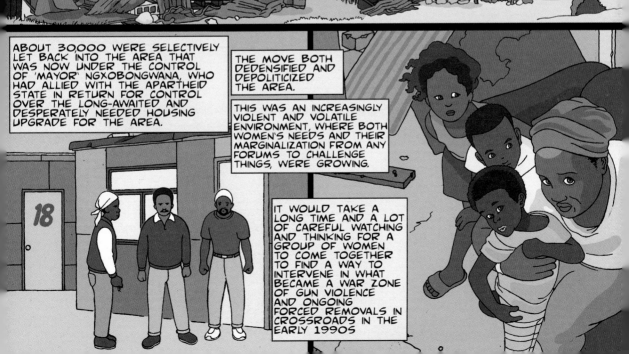

ABOUT 30,000 WERE SELECTIVELY LET BACK INTO THE AREA THAT WAS NOW UNDER THE CONTROL OF 'MAYOR' NGXOBONGWANA, WHO HAD ALLIED WITH THE APARTHEID STATE IN RETURN FOR CONTROL OVER THE LONG-AWAITED AND DESPERATELY NEEDED HOUSING UPGRADE FOR THE AREA.

THE MOVE BOTH DEDENSIFIED AND DEPOLITICIZED THE AREA.

THIS WAS AN INCREASINGLY VIOLENT AND VOLATILE ENVIRONMENT, WHERE BOTH WOMEN'S NEEDS AND THEIR MARGINALIZATION FROM ANY FORUMS TO CHALLENGE THINGS, WERE GROWING.

IT WOULD TAKE A LONG TIME AND A LOT OF CAREFUL WATCHING AND THINKING FOR A GROUP OF WOMEN TO COME TOGETHER TO FIND A WAY TO INTERVENE IN WHAT BECAME A WAR ZONE OF GUN VIOLENCE AND ONGOING FORCED REMOVALS IN CROSSROADS IN THE EARLY 1990S

THIS ENVIRONMENT WAS NOT UNIQUE TO CROSSROADS AT THIS TIME. VIOLENT CONFLICT WAS ON THE RISE NATIONALLY.

POLITICAL PARTIES HAD BEEN UNBANNED AND NATIONAL LEVEL NEGOTIATIONS FOR 'TRANSITION' TO DEMOCRACY WERE TAKING PLACE.

THE STAKES OF THE TALKS WERE EXTREMELY HIGH AND THERE WERE MANY SIDES WITHIN THE SIDES COMPETING TO INFLUENCE THE DIRECTION SOUTH AFRICA WOULD TAKE AND THE NEW TERMS OF ENGAGEMENT TO BE ESTABLISHED.

WOULD THE CALL FOR 'LAND FOR THOSE WHO WORK IT' AND 'HOUSES FOR ALL' SPELLED OUT IN THE FREE- DOM CHARTER MAKE IT ONTO THE NEGOTIATION TABLES? WOULD POWER BE SHARED? WOULD RESOURCES BE REDISTRIBUTED? HOW WOULD UNDERGROUND MOVEMENTS BE DEMOBILIZED AND UNDERGROUND FIGHTERS DECOMMISSIONED? WHO WOULD THE NEW LEADERS BE?

MANY STRUGGLES HAD BEEN CONTAINED WITHIN COMMUNITIES THROUGH THE SUCCESS OF APARTHEID BLACK LOCAL AUTHORITY SYSTEMS AND THEIR LOW INTENSITY CONFLICT STRATEGIES OF THE 1980S. ADDED TO THIS NOW WERE THE INCREASING TENSIONS OVER REDEFINING A NEW PECKING ORDER.

BETWEEN 1990 AND 1994 MORE PEOPLE WERE KILLED IN COMMUNITY STRUGGLES THAT THE STATE LABELLED 'BLACK ON BLACK' VIOLENCE THAN BY THE APARTHEID STATE IN ALL OF THE 1980S.

IN CROSSROADS THESE TENSIONS PLAYED OUT IN A DECADE OF 1990S VIOLENT CONFLICT OVER HOUSING ALLOCATION THAT LOOKED NOTHING LIKE THE IMAGES OF CELEBRATION WITH MANDELA'S RELEASE FROM PRISON, OR THE RAINBOW NATIONALISM OF THE YEARS SURROUNDING THE FIRST DEMOCRATIC ELECTIONS IN SOUTH AFRICA IN 1994.

THE GOLDSTONE COMMISSION WAS EVENTUALLY APPOINTED TO LOOK INTO THE CAUSES OF THIS INCREASED VIOLENCE THAT TOOK PLACE ACROSS THE COUNTRY.

CROSSROADS WAS ONE OF THE PLACES STUDIED BY THE COMMISSION AND THE TESTIMONY OF PEOPLE THERE AND REPORTS OF ORGANIZATIONS THAT WORKED IN THE AREA, LIKE THE TRAUMA CENTRE, UNPACKS A VERY DIFFICULT ENVIRONMENT WHERE WOMEN WERE THREATENED WHEN 4 THEY TRIED TO ORGANIZE, AND FELT LIKE THEIR VOICES WERE 'KEPT IN A TIN.'

LUCKY STAR

PILCHARDS
IN TOMATO SAUCE

IN 1987, 847 BESTER HOMES WENT ON SALE IN CROSSROADS. BEYOND THE MEANS OF MOST SHACK-DWELLERS IN THE AREA, MANY WERE PURCHASED BY RESIDENTS FROM THE MORE ESTABLISHED TOWNSHIPS OF LANGA, NYANGA AND GUGULETHU.

THE FIRST SUBSIDIZED LOW-COST HOUSES, IN A SECTION NAMED UNATHI, WERE BUILT LATER THAT YEAR. THESE HOUSES WERE REFERRED TO AS PHASE 2 OF CROSSROADS' DEVELOPMENT.

IN ORDER TO BUILD THESE HOUSES, PEOPLE IN SECTION 2 WERE MOVED TO A 'TEMPORARY' TRANSIT CAMP WITHIN CROSSROADS; A PIECE OF LAND NORTH OF KLIPFONTEIN ROAD, AGAINST THE N2 HIGHWAY, WHICH BECAME KNOWN AS BOY'S TOWN (NAMED FOR THE 'JUVENILE DELINQUENT' CENTRE THAT USED TO BE THERE).

AS THE FIRST AFFORDABLE HOUSING BUILT IN CROSSROADS AND WITH LESS THAN 900 UNITS, A FIERCE FIGHT BROKE OUT OVER WHO WOULD GET AN UNATHI HOUSE.

THE 'ROLL-OVER' METHOD OF TURNING INFORMAL SETTLEMENTS INTO TOWNSHIPS HAS BEEN WIDELY CRITICIZED FOR THE WAY IT DISPLACES PEOPLE, BECAUSE MOST SHACK AREAS ARE MORE POPULATED THAN THE NEW DEVELOPMENT WILL ALLOW.

UNATHI MEANS PEACE IN ISIXHOSA BUT THE HISTORY OF THIS DEVELOPMENT WAS FAR FROM PEACEFUL.

RELOCATION OF PEOPLE IN UNATHI CONSTITUTED ANOTHER CONTENTIOUS AND BLOODY SET OF 'REMOVALS' AND SHIFTING ALLEGIANCES.

THE TOWN COUNCIL (OF WHICH NGXOBONGWANA WAS THEN THE MAYOR) DECIDED TO ALLOCATE THE HOUSES ACCORDING TO THREE CRITERIA.

FIRST THE APPLICANT HAD TO PROVE TO BE A BONA FIDE INHABITANT OF CROSS-ROADS. SECOND, THEY HAD TO HAVE SETTLED UNPAID SERVICE CHARGES IN FULL. THIRD, PREFER- ENCE WAS TO BE GIVEN TO APPLICANTS WHO WERE INHABITANTS OF BOYS TOWN.

WHILE THESE REQUIREMENTS WERE CALCULATED TO ENSURE THAT ONLY SECTION 2 RESIDENTS CLAIMED UNATHI HOUSES, THEY ALSO EXCLUDED MOST SECTION 2 RESIDENTS BECAUSE MOST INHABITANTS OF BOYS TOWN WERE HEAVILY IN ARREARS.

BOYS TOWN RESIDENTS ARGUED THAT THEY HAD BEEN INTIMIDATED BY NGXOBONGWANA IN THE PAST NOT TO PAY SERVICE CHARGES AS PART OF RESISTANCE TO APARTHEID.

THE GOLDSTONE COMMISSION CONCLUDES THAT: IT GOES WITHOUT SAYING THAT HAD THE PEOPLE OF BOYS TOWN WHO WERE ENTITLED TO THEIR HOUSES BEEN PROPERLY CONSULTED AND HAD THEY BEEN GIVEN A SAY IN THE DECISION AS TO THE ALLO-CATION OF HOUSES, THEY WOULD HARDLY HAVE MADE IT A PREREQUISITE THAT ARREAR SERVICE CHARGES HAD TO BE PAID IN FULL.

THREE WEEKS AFTER THE HOUSES WERE READY THERE WERE STILL NO APPLICANTS AND THE HOUSES WERE BEING STONED BY PEOPLE FROM BOYS TOWN, ALBEIT FOR DIFFERENT REASONS.

THE GOLDSTONE COMMISSION RECORDS THAT 'DUE TO INCREASING VANDALISM' OF THE HOUSES IT WAS DECIDED TO OFFER THE HOUSES TO ALL REGISTERED INHABITANTS OF CROSSROADS.

BUT RESIDENTS FROM SECTION 4 OF OLD CROSSROADS ARGUED THAT RENTS WERE TOO HIGH AND UNDER THE LEADERSHIP OF JEFFREY NONGWE, ONE OF NGXOBONGWANA'S DISSIDENT HEADMEN, THEY URGED OTHER SHACK DWELLERS NOT TO OCCUPY THE HOUSES.

WHEN SOME PEOPLE MOVED IN, NONGWE'S PEOPLE STONED THE HOUSES.

PEOPLE FROM BOYS TOWN TOOK PART IN THE STONING OUT OF FRUSTRATION WITH THE UNCLEAR ALLOCATION PROCESS AND A SENSE OF ANGER THAT 'OUTSIDERS' WERE BEING ACCOMMODATED AND THAT CORRUPTION WAS AT PLAY.

THEY ALSO BELIEVED THAT SOME PEOPLE TOOK ADVANTAGE OF THE DISPUTE TO OCCUPY THE HOUSES ON THEIR OWN WITHOUT COUNCIL OFFICE PERMISSION.

UNATHI WAS THE FIRST AND LAST AFFORDABLE HOUSING BUILT IN CROSSROADS UNDER APARTHEID. FEWER THAN 900 UNITS COULD NOT BEGIN TO TOUCH THE TIP OF THE ICEBERG IN CROSSROADS WHERE 30,000 PEOPLE WERE SAID TO BE LIVING IN SHACKS IN 1991.

WHILE NO HOUSES WERE BUILT BETWEEN 1988 AND 1998, RELOCATION CONTINUED. DURING THIS TIME PEOPLE IN CROSSROADS HAD NO CHOICE BUT TO PUT THEIR SUPPORT BEHIND ONE OF THE FEW MEN IN POSITIONS OF POLITICAL LEADERSHIP.

THERE WAS NO WAY TO ESCAPE THE WAY HOUSING POLITICS PLAYED OUT IN CROSSROADS IN THE 1990S.

MR. TOMSANA:

I WAS PERCEIVED TO BE ON NONGWE'S SIDE IN 1990, WHICH WAS ALSO SEEN BY SOME TO MEAN THE 'COMRADES' AND THE 'YOUTH.'

AS A RESULT HIS 16-YEAR-OLD SON WAS KILLED WHILE LOOKING FOR HIS FATHER DURING A MAJOR MEETING HELD AT THE UNIVERSITY OF THE WESTERN CAPE FOR THE PURPOSES OF 'RECONCILING' SIDES.

HIS FAMILY WAS ALLOCATED A HOUSE IN UNATHI IN 1991 BUT FEARED TO TAKE UP RESIDENCE.

HIS DAUGHTER, NOMANDLA, WHO HAD BEEN DELIVERED IN A SHACK BY THE ACTIVIST ANGLICAN PRIEST, FATHER RUSSELL, IN CROSSROADS IN THE MIDST OF A MASSIVE RAID IN THE 1970S, EXPLAINED:

SOME OF THESE UNATHI HOUSES WERE VANDALIZED BY THE PEOPLE OF NONGWE WHO DIDN'T WANT PEOPLE TO STAY HERE.

BUT THEN THE FOLLOWING YEAR THE TOMSANAS'S SHACK WAS RAZED TO THE GROUND WHEN SECTION 2 WAS BURNT OUT. THEY HAD TO MOVE AGAIN.

THE FAMILY SPLIT UP, STAYING WITH EXTENDED FAMILY SPREAD ACROSS CROSSROADS.

MANY PEOPLE FLED THE VIOLENCE AND THEIR HOUSES WERE OCCUPIED BY OTHER PEOPLE.

JULIA MATISO SAID THAT SHE LEFT IN 1991 AND TOOK REFUGE IN PLASTIC SHELTERS. AFTER THE FIGHTS SHE WAS AFRAID BECAUSE

QUEEN SHUGU RETURNED AT THE END OF THE FIGHTING AND CLOSED HER HOUSE WITH CORRUGATED IRON AND ZINC TO PROTECT THE HOUSE, WHICH SHE WAS STILL FEARFUL TO MOVE INTO.

...THE HOUSE WAS ISOLATED AND I WAS ON MY OWN BY THEN.

THESE DAMAGED HOUSES BECAME KNOWN AS AMABHODLO (DILAPIDATED/ STONED) AND LATER REPORTS WOULD SHOW THAT 'NO STRICT MEASURES WERE TAKEN TO CURB THE FORCEFUL OCCUPATION OF AMABHODLO.'

OVER 100 HOUSES WERE DESTROYED AND TENS OF PEOPLE KILLED IN THE 1991 CONFLICT, ACCORDING TO THE TRUTH AND RECONCILIATION COMMISSION.

IN 1988 ELECTIONS TOOK PLACE IN CROSSROADS AND NGXOBONGWANA WAS ELECTED MAYOR WITH 21 HEADMEN OVERSEEN BY HIS NEW CHAIRMAN, JEFFREY NONGWE.

A SPLIT BETWEEN THE TWO MEN BEGAN IN LATE 1989 WHEN NONGWE ACCUSED NGXOBONGWANA OF SELLING BESTER HOUSES TO OUTSIDERS, SELLING LAND TO BANKS AND OF UNFAIR ALLOCATION IN UNATHI.

NONGWE ALSO ACCUSED NGXOBONGWANA OF NOT FULFILLING HIS PROMISE TO BUILD HOUSES FOR THOSE PEOPLE WHO MOVED FROM SECTION 4 TO BOYS TOWN.

NONGWE AND 14 HEADMEN SPLIT, PRECIPITATING 'OPEN WARFARE' THAT LASTED SEVERAL MONTHS WITH MANY WOUNDED AND KILLED AND HOUSES BURNT.

CONFLICT ESCALATED BETWEEN THE TWO GROUPS AND IN OCTOBER 1990 NGXOBONGWANA AND 2000 OF HIS FOLLOWERS WERE OUSTED AND RELOCATED THEMSELVES TO DRIFT-SANDS (AN OPEN SPACE OF SAND DUNE ADJACENT TO KHAYELITSHA).

DURING THIS CONFLICT, SECTION 1 WAS COMPLETELY RAZED TO THE GROUND.

MAMA TEN TEN WAS ONE OF THE WOMEN WHO FLED TO DRIFTSANDS WITH NGXOBONGWANA:

IN 1990 THERE WERE FIGHTS IN CROSSROADS AMONGST OUR NINE HEADMEN.

THEY EACH HAD A SECTION. NONGWE IN SECTION 1, NGXOBONGWANA, MAZELE WHO HAS PASSED NOW, VETWANI, TIWANE WHO HAS PASSED NOW, MBIZA WHO LIVES SOMEWHERE IN KHAYELITSHA NOW.

HOUSES WERE BURNT AND PEOPLE WERE SHOT DEAD.

'THE ONE THING I CANNOT EXPLAIN ABOUT CROSSROADS ARE THE FIGHTS. I WILL NEVER GO BACK. I HAVE NEVER GONE THERE SINCE 1990 AND I NEVER WILL. I DON'T WANT TO KNOW ABOUT CROSSROADS.'

SELENA DASI DESCRIBES HOW NGXOBONGWANA'S SHIFTS IN ALLEGIANCE LED TO NONGWE'S CHALLENGE TO HIM AS A COUNCILLOR:

IN 1989 UPROAR ERUPTED BETWEEN THE GROUPS OF NGXOBONGWANA AND NONGWE. THEY WERE KILLING EACH OTHER.

'IF YOU ARE A PARTISAN OF NGXOBONGWANA, NONGWE'S SUPPORTERS WILL BURN YOUR HOUSE.'

'SO MY HOUSE WAS BURNT DOWN AND THEN I CAME TO STAY HERE AND OPENED UP A SMALL BUSINESS.'

'I WAS SLEEPING AT A GARAGE WITH MY MOTHER AND CHILDREN...'

'AT THE BEGINNING NGXOBONGWANA WAS A GREAT LEADER WHO STOOD FOR PEOPLE'S RIGHTS. WHITE PEOPLE WERE ALSO SCARED OF HIM.'

'IF HE SEES THEM IT WAS AS IF HE SAW ANIMALS.'

LIKE NGXOBONGWANA'S IMPACT ON THE UNITED DEMOCRATIC FRONT (UDF) AFFILIATES IN THE 1980S, MANY ARGUE THAT NONGWE 'POISONED THE ANC NAME' IN CROSSROADS IN THE 1990S. HE RECEIVED BACKING FROM THE APARTHEID STATE AFTER NGXOBONGWANA WAS CHASED OUT AND AT THE SAME TIME PUT UP AN ANC FLAG AND DECLARED HIMSELF ANC CHAIRMAN AND CHAIR OF THE WESTERN CAPE UNITED SQUATTER ASSOCIATION (WECUSA).

NONGWE JUXTAPOSED HIMSELF TO NGXOBONGWANA'S 'CORRUPTION,' DESPITE SHOWING FEW SIGNS OF ADHERING TO THE ANC'S PHILOSOPHY OF HUMAN RIGHTS AND DEMOCRACY.

DESPITE COMPLAINTS ABOUT NONGWE TO THE ANC DATING BACK TO 1991 HE WAS ONLY SUSPENDED FROM THE PARTY IN 1993.

THUS A SECOND ANC BRANCH WAS OPENED IN CROSSROADS. IT WAS BASED IN UNATHI AND CALLED THE BUNTUBAKHE ANC BRANCH, WHICH RESULTED IN A DECREASE IN NONGWE'S SUPPORT.

ELESE DEPOUTCH, NICKNAMED WHITEY, AN MK-TRAINED ACTIVIST WHO HAD RETURNED TO THE WESTERN CAPE, MOVED TO UNATHI WHERE HE WAS INVOLVED IN SETTING UP THE BRANCH IN 1991.

OTHER PARTIES, LIKE THE SACP, BEGAN ESTABLISHING BRANCHES IN CROSSROADS AS WELL.

BETWEEN 1990 AND 1992 THE CAPE PROVINCIAL AUTHORITY (CPA) EMPOWERED NONGWE WITH CONTROL OVER 'UPGRADING.' THEY REGARDED HIM AS THE POPULAR LEADER AND HE WAS THE ONLY ONE CONSULTED.

THEY EXPECTED HIM TO INFORM HIS FOLLOWERS ABOUT THE PLANS AND TO PERSUADE THEM TO MOVE VOLUNTARILY TO TEMPORARY ALTERNATIVE SITES AT LOWER CROSSROADS. THE CPA ALSO EMPOWERED NONGWE TO APPOINT LABOURERS AND PRIVATE CONTRACTORS TO ASSIST IN THE RESETTLEMENT OF PEOPLE FROM CROSSROADS.

THESE RESETTLEMENTS WERE DONE BY FORCE, AND VIOLENCE INCREASED BETWEEN MARCH TO JUNE 1993. THE CONFLICT WAS CONCENTRATED BETWEEN NONGWE AND HIS FOLLOWERS ON ONE HAND AND THE PEOPLE OF SECTIONS 2 AND 3 ON THE OTHER. THE HORRIFIC DETAILS OF THIS 'WAR' WHICH BEGAN IN MARCH 1993, INTENSIFIED IN APRIL AND EASED IN JUNE WHEN MOST OF SECTIONS 2 AND 3 WERE DESTROYED, ARE CAPTURED IN THE PRESS AND IN THE SUBMISSIONS TO THE GOLDSTONE COMMISSION BY THE TRAUMA CENTRE FOR VICTIMS OF VIOLENCE AND TORTURE.

DISPLACED PEOPLE DESCRIBED THE EXPERIENCE:

'I FLED THE AREA WITH MY CHILDREN ON APRIL 15, AFTER THE BURNINGS. ALL WE HAVE LEFT ARE OUR TWO MATTRESSES. NOTHING ELSE. I STILL FEEL SHOCK AND AM NOT SLEEPING.'

'MY FATHER WAS SHOT. HE HAS BEEN HOSPITALIZED FOR THREE WEEKS. MY MOTHER HAS BEEN IN HIDING EVER SINCE.'

NOT ONLY WERE PEOPLE CHASED AWAY BUT THEY COULD NOT TAKE ANY OF THEIR SHACK MATERIALS WITH THEM.

NGXOBONGWANA'S DEPARTURE FROM THE AREA DID NOT DECREASE VIOLENT CONFLICT. THE TRC ARGUED THAT THE UNATHI CONFLICT HIGHLIGHTED THE WAYS IN WHICH THE UNDEMOCRATIC HEADMEN AND HOMEGUARD STYLE OF POLITICAL CONTROL WAS BEING REPLICATED IN THE ANC IN CROSSROADS IN THE 1990S.

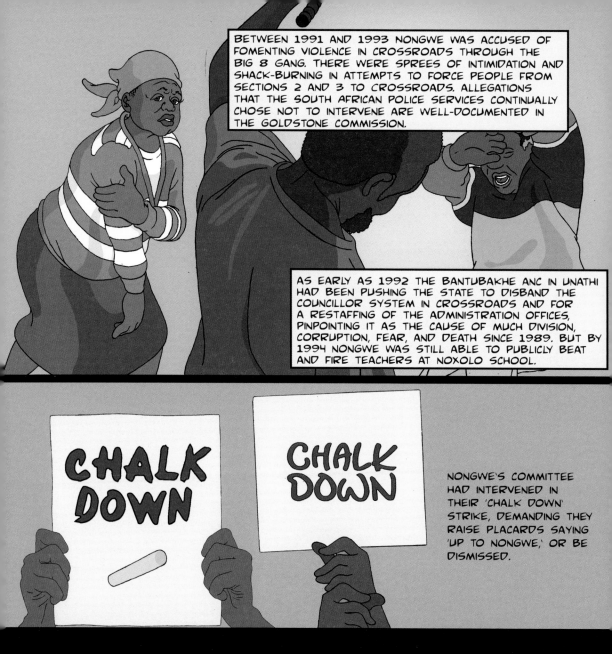

BETWEEN 1991 AND 1993 NONGWE WAS ACCUSED OF FOMENTING VIOLENCE IN CROSSROADS THROUGH THE BIG 8 GANG. THERE WERE SPREES OF INTIMIDATION AND SHACK-BURNING IN ATTEMPTS TO FORCE PEOPLE FROM SECTIONS 2 AND 3 TO CROSSROADS. ALLEGATIONS THAT THE SOUTH AFRICAN POLICE SERVICES CONTINUALLY CHOSE NOT TO INTERVENE ARE WELL-DOCUMENTED IN THE GOLDSTONE COMMISSION.

AS EARLY AS 1992 THE BANTUBAKHE ANC IN UNATHI HAD BEEN PUSHING THE STATE TO DISBAND THE COUNCILLOR SYSTEM IN CROSSROADS AND FOR A RESTAFFING OF THE ADMINISTRATION OFFICES, PINPOINTING IT AS THE CAUSE OF MUCH DIVISION, CORRUPTION, FEAR, AND DEATH SINCE 1989. BUT BY 1994 NONGWE WAS STILL ABLE TO PUBLICLY BEAT AND FIRE TEACHERS AT NOXOLO SCHOOL.

CHALK DOWN

CHALK DOWN

NONGWE'S COMMITTEE HAD INTERVENED IN THEIR 'CHALK DOWN' STRIKE, DEMANDING THEY RAISE PLACARDS SAYING 'UP TO NONGWE,' OR BE DISMISSED.

UP NONGW

UP NONGWE

TEACHERS ACCUSED HIS COMMITTEE OF 'BULLYING' AND 'DICTATING' DURING MEETINGS, DESPITE HAVING NO ELECTED POSITIONS FROM PARENTS OR TEACHERS.

TEACHERS ALSO REPORTED A TIME WHEN HE 'SJAMBOKED AND SLAPPED THEM IN FRONT OF THE SCHOOL CHILDREN.'

CHRIS HANI

Socialism is the Future

THE TRAUMA CENTRE ARGUED THAT THESE ATTACKS WERE 'NOT COINCIDENTALLY DURING THE GENERAL UNREST WHICH TOOK PLACE FOLLOWING THE ASSASSINATION OF CHRIS HANI.'

THE CENTRE ARGUED THAT THIS WAS NOT RANDOM IRRATIONAL VIOLENCE BUT RATIONAL AND ORGANIZED TO A CERTAIN DEGREE, PLANNED TO ACHIEVE PARTICULAR OBJECTIVES. VIOLENCE WAS USED IN AN ORGANIZED FASHION TO CLEAR SECTIONS 2 AND 3 TO MAKE WAY FOR UPGRADING.

PRESS ARTICLES DEPICTED THE WAR ZONE. PHOTOGRAPHS SHOWED GROUPS OF MEN CARRYING AXES AND STATE MILITARY VEHICLES AND CASSPIRS IN CROSSROADS.

THE ATTACKS WERE POINTED AND A DIRECT RESPONSE TO PEOPLE REFUSING TO MOVE.

TESTIMONY PROVIDED AT THE GOLDSTONE COMMISSION:

'I WAS ACCUSED OF INSTIGATING THE PEOPLE NOT TO MOVE OUT OF CROSSROADS, AGAINST NONGWE'S INSTRUCTIONS.'

'ON APRIL 15 I SAW MY SHACK WAS ALREADY BURNT TO THE GROUND. I LATER LEARNED THAT MY WIFE HAD BEEN BEATEN AND ATTACKED. THEY EVEN SHOT MY DOG AND THREW IT BACK INTO THE BURNING SHACK.'

BY JULY 1993 OVER 800 PEOPLE
(OVER HALF OF WHOM WERE CHILDREN)
HAD BEEN DIRECTLY AFFECTED BY
ACTS OF POLITICAL VIOLENCE SINCE THE
BEGINNING OF MARCH. THIS INCLUDED:

126 arsons in which people lost their homes and possessions; 50 cases of people abandoning their homes and fleeing Crossroads because of violence and intimidation; 82 cases of attempted murder, resulting in serious injuries and, in some cases, permanent disability; at least 48 murders, nearly all men, nearly all breadwinners in their families; a minimum of 10.

DURING THIS VIOLENCE NONGWE DEFECTORS FLED SECTION 4 IN 1993, THEY WENT TO STAY WITH FAMILIES ELSEWHERE IN CROSSROADS AND IN PARTICULAR THEY WERE TAKEN IN BY WOMEN IN UNATHI.

THESE WERE YOUNGSTERS ESCAPING THE TROUBLE BETWEEN NONGWE AND YOUTH, WHICH MEANT THAT NOW WOMEN WERE DIRECTLY INVOLVED. VIOLENCE FROM EVERY QUARTER ESCALATED.

PIECING TOGETHER WHO WAS PUSHED WHERE IS VERY DIFFICULT. FOR EXAMPLE, DURING THIS TIME MANY PEOPLE HAD BEEN CHASED TO SECTION 4 WHEN A BLOODY PUTSCH REMOVED MR. TOISE FROM HIS LEADERSHIP IN BROWN'S FARM. 75 PEOPLE STAYED AT THE NYANGA POLICE STATION FOR THREE WEEKS BEFORE THEY FINALLY TOOK REFUGE WITH NONGWE IN SECTION 4 LIVING 'UNDER EXTREMELY HARSH CONDITIONS.'

IT IS ALSO IMPOSSIBLE TO EXTRAPOLATE WHO WAS IN THE 'RIGHT' OR IN THE 'WRONG' DURING THIS TIME. THE TRAUMA CENTRE DESCRIBES A SITUATION WHEREBY 'THE VICTIMS BECAME THE PERPETRATORS OF VIOLENCE IN SELF-DEFENSE AND THE PERPETRATORS BECAME THE VICTIMS.'

IT WAS IN THIS CONTEXT THAT A GROUP OF WOMEN FORMED THE MOTHERS OF CROSSROADS, IN AN ATTEMPT TO BRING ATTENTION TO THE WAY THESE FORCED REMOVALS WERE BEING DONE WITH FORCE AND INCITING VIOLENCE.

THEY ATTEMPTED TO PUSH FOR PEACE AND PROTECT YOUTH WHO WERE TRYING TO GET OUT OF SECTION 4 WHERE VIOLENCE ENGULFED CROSSROADS IN 1993.

MAMA HAMSE:

THE PEOPLE OF UNATHI WERE KILLED BY PEOPLE OF SECTION 4. EVEN THIS VIOLENCE ERUPTED AMONGST THE YOUNGSTERS. THEY KILLED EACH OTHER IN THE DAM.

SINCE 1991 JOYCE NDINISE ELESE HAD CALLED UPON THE BLACK SASH AS HER FAMILY WAS CONSTANTLY HARASSED BY THE SECURITY FORCES DUE TO THE INVOLVEMENT OF HER NEPHEW, ELESE DEPOUTCH, WHO WOULD LATER BECOME THE ANC COUNCILLOR OF CROSSROADS.

WOMEN APPROACHING THE BLACK SASH ONLY IRRITATED NONGWE.

FINDING LITTLE SOLUTION TO THE GUN VIOLENCE IN THE AREA, CROSSROADS WOMEN WERE JOINED BY WOMEN IN THE SURROUNDING NYANGA AREA TO JOIN FORCES IN SEARCH OF SOLUTIONS. THIS WAS THE FIRST TIME IN AGES THAT NEIGHBOURS IN NYANGA DARED TO GET INVOLVED. ALMOST A DECADE AFTER WITDOEKE, VETERAN LEADERS LIKE MAMA NTONGANA, LIVING IN NEW CROSSROADS, WOULD NO MORE HAVE CROSSED INTO OLD CROSSROADS TERRITORY THAN A GANG MEMBER IN CHICAGO WOULD HAVE PENETRATED INTO SOME OTHER

MAMA HAMSE EXPLAINS HOW THE WOMEN'S PEACE MOVEMENT WAS FORMED:

'I WAS A MEMBER OF THE WOMEN'S PEACE ORGANIZATION AT MFESANE WITH MR. DESMOND TUTU AND MRS. LEYA. I WILL TELL YOU WHY... THERE WAS A SURGE OF VIOLENCE AROUND HERE, EVEN IN LOWER CROSSROAD.'

'MANY PEOPLE DIED AND I HAD TO GO TO LOWER CROSSROAD BECAUSE I USED TO LIVE WITH SOME OF THEM HERE IN SECTION 1.'

'WE SEPARATED BECAUSE OF THE FORCED REMOVALS. I ASKED THE BLACK SASH TO INTERFERE WHEN WE HAD PROBLEMS. THEN MRS. NGUNWAYO, SKOTI AND VAAL CHRISTIE USED TO ATTEND THE MEETINGS.'

1994 HAD NOT BROUGHT PEACE TO CROSSROADS:

'SOME OF THE HOUSES WERE BURNT AND THEY APPROACHED RED CROSS TO SUPPLY THEM WITH FOOD AND CLOTHES.'

'WE USED TO HAVE SOME MEETINGS TO GET THEM TO BE PART OF THE ORGANIZATION SO THAT WE CAN TRY TO CREATE PEACE AMONGST WOMEN. SO WE USED TO HOLD MEETINGS WITH WOMEN AT THE NYANGA PRESBYTERIAN CHURCH.'

'THEN WE ASKED ANOTHER GUY CALLED ROMAN FROM THE EASTERN CAPE TO HAVE SOME WORKSHOPS WITH US. THE AIM OF THE WORKSHOPS WAS TO UNITE PEOPLE BECAUSE THE HOUSES BY THAT TIME WERE DEMOLISHED. SO VIOLENCE WAS STILL BREWING AT THAT TIME.'

ERMC

THE MOTHERS OF CROSSROADS APPROACHED OUTSIDE ORGANIZATIONS
BUT UNLIKE IN EARLIER DECADES THEY FOUND LITTLE LASTING SUCCESS.

WITHDRAWAL OF OUTSIDE ORGANIZATIONS HAD BEGUN IN THE MID-1980S.
BUT WOMEN PUSHED TO FIND OUTSIDE SUPPORT AND BY 1993 THEY
FOUND ENCOURAGEMENT FROM CONCERNED INDIVIDUALS FROM VARIOUS
CONFLICT RESOLUTION AND WOMEN NGOS.

FROM MARCH 1993 THE TRAUMA CENTRE BEGAN TO CONVENE WEEKLY
MEETINGS WITH SOCIAL SERVICE AGENCIES, PEACE MONITORS, AND
CHURCH GROUPS TO SHARE INFORMATION ON VICTIMS OF VIOLENCE.

THIS INCLUDED THE RED CROSS, SHAWCO, THE LOCAL PEACE COMMITTEE,
VARIOUS MONITORS, AND THE BLACK SASH. THESE GROUPS WERE
SKEPTICAL OF WHAT WOULD CONSTITUTE THE MOST APPROPRIATE AND
POSSIBLE ASSISTANCE IN CROSSROADS AT THAT TIME.

IN 1993 CROSSROADS WOMEN SET UP A ROOM TO COLLECT FOOD
AND CLOTHES. DESPITE THEIR ENERGY FOR COMMUNITY ORGANIZING,
WHEN THEY ASKED THE BLACK SASH TO RUN THE ROOM TO
DISTRIBUTE FOOD AND CLOTHES, THE SASH DECLINED.

IT WAS A TIME WHEN 'THE CIVICS WERE NOT ALLOWED TO BE STRONG
AND OUTSIDE ORGANIZATIONS WERE HESITANT TO GET INVOLVED YET
SAW THE NEED.'

IN THIS DIFFICULT ENVIRONMENT, MOTHERS OF CROSSROADS CONSTITUTED THEMSELVES INTO A PROACTIVE GROUP FOR SELF-EMPOWERMENT AND HAD PROCEEDED TO EMBARK ON RED CROSS HOME-CARE COURSES, FOLLOWED BY EDUCARE TRAINING SO THAT SOME OF THEIR MEMBERS WERE ABLE TO OPEN CRECHES ATTACHED TO THEIR HOMES AND GET FOOD SUBSIDY GRANTS.

THE MOTHERS OF CROSSROADS WAS INITIATED OUT OF CONCERN FOR YOUTH BEING KILLED IN THE HOUSING CONFLICT AND EXTENDED TO EDUCATING AND FEEDING CHILDREN.

THEY ALSO STRATEGIZED ABOUT HOW TO INTERVENE IN PEACE POLITICS, INCLUDING PUSHING FOR AN ENQUIRY INTO THE CONFLICT.

MAMA HAMSE: 'WE APPROACHED WOMEN FROM LOWER CROSSROADS AND PEOPLE FROM BOYS TOWN TO TEACH THEM FIRST AID TRAINING THIS WAS OUR FIRST STEP. THEY RECEIVED FIRST AID CERTIFICATES AND AFTER THAT WE HAD MEETINGS AT MFESANE. THE AIMS OF THE WORKSHOP WERE FOR WOMEN TO HAVE PRESCHOOLS AND GARDENS, AND SOME MUST BE INVOLVED IN SEWING.'

JUST AS WOMEN WERE GAINING MOMENTUM, JOYCE NDINISE ELESE WAS KILLED ON MARCH 19, 1993, WHEN MASKED GUNMEN BURST INTO HER HOUSE, ALLEGEDLY LOOKING FOR HER NEPHEW.

ANNE GREENWELL: 'HER DEATH PLAYED A KEY ROLE IN DEFLATING WOMEN'S MOBILIZING AS THE PRICE OF STANDING OUT AS AN INITIATOR OF ALTERNATIVES WAS CLEARLY VERY HIGH.'

JOYCE ELESE WOULD HAVE BEEN THE BACKBONE OF THE MOTHERS OF CROSSROADS BUT HER MURDER IN MARCH WAS THE FINAL STRAW IN ESCALATION OF VIOLENCE. OTHER KEY LEADERS WERE INTIMIDATED. MAMA DASI FOR EXAMPLE WAS CHASED TO KHAYELITSHA. IN RESPONSE TO NDINISE'S DEATH THE MOTHERS WENT TO LOCAL CIVICS, TO FORCE THE ISSUE AND TO GET ACTION.

THE MOTHERS OF CROSSROADS WENT TO THE PROVINCE AND DEMANDED AN ENQUIRY. THEY TOOK BIG RISKS GIVING STATEMENTS BEFORE THE COMMISSION. THIS WAS AN IMPORTANT TURNING POINT IN TENSIONS WITHIN CROSSROADS THAT THESE WOMEN NEVER RECEIVED ENOUGH RECOGNITION FOR.

THE GOLDSTONE COMMISSION DEPICTED A SCENARIO WHERE NO ORGANIZED GROUPS HAD BOTH THE POWER AND THE WILL TO PUT AN END TO THE ARMED CONFLICT IN THE AREA:

'Violence and intimidation was of such a nature and degree that law enforcement in the area proved to be ineffectual, and efforts at peace-brokering by various groups such as the Local Peace Committee, the Network of Independent Monitors, the Black Sash and the local branch of the ANC was rendered futile.'

IT WAS AGAINST THIS BACKDROP THAT THE COMMISSION ANNOUNCED ON JUNE 18, 1993, THAT AN INQUIRY INTO THE CAUSE AND NATURE OF THE VIOLENCE AND INTIMIDATION WOULD BE HELD BY A COMMITTEE OF THE COMMISSION.

MAMA HAMSE: 'WE WENT TO THE GOLDSTONE COMMISSION AND LAID THE PROBLEM ON THE TABLE AND WE HAD A MARCH AROUND CROSSROADS WITH ALLAN BOESAK AND DESMOND TUTU.'

SUSAN CODJWA, MOTHER OF CROSSROADS MEMBER.

ANNE GREENWELL, BLACK SASH AND QUAKER PEACE MOVEMENT CROSSROADS VOLUNTEER.

WHILE IT WAS QUITE A FEAT AND A MOMENT OF POTENTIAL CHANGE TO BE ABLE TO GO INTO SECTION 4 AND TAKE STATEMENTS, INCLUDING THAT OF NONGWE, IT DID NOT STICK.

1994 CAME AND WENT IN AN ATMOSPHERE OF ONGOING TENSION. IT WAS ONLY IN MARCH 1995 THAT A PEACE DECLARATION WAS SIGNED BETWEEN SECTION 2, 4, BOYS TOWN, NEW REST, UNATHI, AND PHASE 1.

MOST BLACK WOMEN IN SOUTH AFRICA EXPERIENCED THE 1980S AS WAR. WHEN SOCIOLOGIST JACKLYN COCK SURVEYED WOMEN IN THE EARLY 1980S AND ASKED IF THERE WAS A WAR GOING ON IN SOUTH AFRICA, SOME WHITE WOMEN SAID YES, AND SOME SAID NO, BUT ALL BLACK WOMEN SHE INTERVIEWED DESCRIBED THE SITUATION IN SOUTH AFRICA AS WAR.

CONFLICT INCREASED IN THE EARLY 1990S ACROSS THE COUNTRY.

IN CROSSROADS WOMEN FELT UNWELCOME TO PARTICIPATE IN POLITICS AND PUBLIC SPACES AS A GROUP, BUT INDIVIDUAL WOMEN CONTINUED TO ATTEMPT TO ENGAGE.

IN JUNE 1994, FOR THE FIRST TIME SINCE SHE FLED CROSSROADS IN THE 1980S, MAMA NTONGANA, THE FIERCE LEADER OF THE PREVIOUS WOMEN'S COMMITTEE, WENT BACK TO VISIT OLD CROSSROADS.

SHE RAN INTO WOMEN SHE KNEW: 'THE WOMEN, THEY WERE CRAZY WHEN THEY SAW ME AND THEY ASKED ME TO HAVE A CHAT WITH THEM. AND I CAN SEE WOMEN ARE FALLING APART NOW. THE STREET WAS SO DIRTY. THE TOILETS WERE BLOCKED. EVERYTHING WAS JUST BROKE.'

THE WOMEN WANTED NTONGANA TO HELP THEM ORGANIZE THEMSELVES. THEY TALKED ABOUT CREATING A CRECHE, ABOUT BEGINNING A DEMONSTRATION, ABOUT CLEANING UP REFUSE IN THE NEIGHBOURHOOD. BUT SIMILAR TO THE MOTHERS OF CROSSROADS' BRIEF SURGE OF ENERGY AND GENERAL FEELING OF BEING SUPPRESSED, THIS INITIATIVE DID NOT BEAR ANY COLLECTIVE FRUIT.

SOUTH AFRICA WAS CELEBRATED FOR ITS LIBERATION
WITHOUT A WAR AND ITS AVOIDANCE OF POST-COLONIAL
CIVIL WARFARE, BUT THIS IGNORES NOT ONLY THE
BLOODSHED AND EXPERIENCES OF DISPLACED PEOPLE
IN CROSSROADS BUT ALSO THE ESTABLISHMENT
OF A SYSTEM THAT WOULD CONTINUE TO BENEFIT
THE WHITE MINORITY AT THE EXPENSE OF THE BLACK
MAJORITY, WELL BEYOND THE APARTHEID ERA.

WITDOEKE PAVED THE WAY FOR A REWRITING OF THE
HISTORY OF CROSSROADS.

IN THE CASE OF OFFICIAL COMMISSIONS ON WITDOEKE, THE
LEADERS WERE HIGHLIGHTED. FOR EXAMPLE, GOLDSTONE
DESCRIBES CROSSROADS' PAST AS FOLLOWS:

'The two leaders in the Crossroads area at the time
of defiance and resistance, J. Ngxobongwana and
O. Memani joined forces and formed the United
Crossroads Committee. This committee
obtained assistance from a variety of
organizations, including the Urban Foundation.
These organizations facilitated discussions
between the then Minister of Cooperation
and Development, Dr. Piet Koornhof and the
Crossroads Committee.'

NO MENTION OF THE WOMEN'S MOBILIZING,
NO MENTION OF THE BLACK SASH, ETC. YET
EVERY SINGLE LEADER OF NGXOBONGWANA'S
OPPOSITION IS NAMED.

THIS NOT ONLY ERASES WOMEN FROM THE PAST, IT ALSO
HIDES HOW THEIR MOBILIZING WAS SPECIFICALLY ATTACKED
AND THEIR ISSUES SILENCED.

Chapter Six

The Women's Power Group

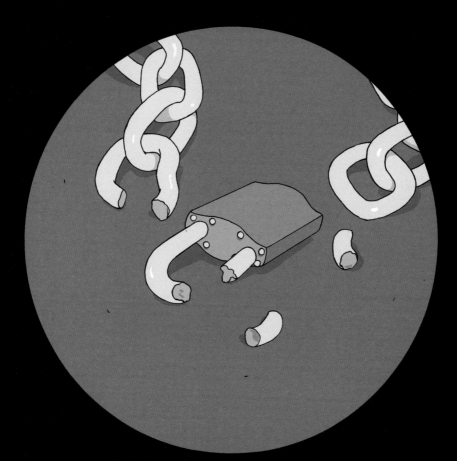

FOUNDED IN 1997, THE WOMEN'S POWER GROUP WAS INITIATED BY WOMEN IN CROSSROADS WHEN NEW SERVICE FEES WERE ANNOUNCED AND WHEN THE SHOW HOUSES OF THE FIRST POST-1994 UNITS WERE COMPLETE.

ON DISPLAY WERE TINY ONE-ROOM HOUSES THAT FELL SHORT OF THE KINDS OF SPACES WOMEN NEEDED TO CREATE HOMES.

THE INITIAL LIST OF ISSUES THAT THEY SAID BROUGHT THEM TOGETHER INCLUDED:

-HOUSING
-REVAMPED SERVICE CHARGES
-MISSING HOUSING FUNDS
-FILTH OF SCHOOLS AND CLINICS
-LACK OF CRÈCHES
-AND THE INABILITY OF THE STATE (COUNCILLORS AND POLICE) TO PROVIDE SECURITY IN CROSSROADS

THEY REJECTED NEWLY PRO-POSED SERVICE CHARGES: 'INCREASED FEES IN RETURN FOR EMPTY PROMISES?!'

MAMA SHUGU: 'THEY ARE PROMISING PEOPLE, BUT THEY ARE NOT DELIVERING.'

WHEN HOUSES WERE BUILT THEY WERE EXTREMELY SMALL, AND WOMEN APPROACHED COUNCILLORS WITH SUGGESTIONS OF WHERE TO FIND FUNDS TO INCREASE THEIR SIZE.

IN 1980/1 AND 1987 RESPECTIVELY, WERE AT LEAST 45 SQ. METERS. THE NEW SHOW HOUSES WERE 35 SQ. METERS.

PARTICULAR SIGNIFICANCE TO WOMEN, WHO REFERRED TO THE PROPOSED HOUSES AS 'VEZA,' WHICH MEANS 'SHOW' IN ISIXHOSA; AS IN VEZA INYAWO, 'SHOWING YOUR FEET.' THE HOUSES WERE SO SMALL THAT WHEN YOU LIE DOWN TO SLEEP YOUR FEET STICK OUT.

NOT ONLY WERE THESE HOUSES TINY BUT THEY WERE OF INFERIOR WORKMANSHIP.

WOMEN HAD BEEN STRUGGLING FOR URBAN SECURITY FOR DECADES AND THE SUBSIDY HOUSES WOULD BE THEIR FIRST AND ONLY HOPE OF DECENT SHELTER.

THE LOCAL RECONSTRUCTION AND DEVELOPMENT PROGRAM FORUM (RDP), ELECTED IN 1996, CLAIMED THAT ONCE BUILDING SITE AND SERVICES INFRASTRUCTURE EXPENSES, AMOUNTING TO R17,000, HAD BEEN DEDUCTED FROM THE ALLOCATED STATE SUBSIDY, ONLY R8500 REMAINED TO SPEND ON THE ACTUAL BUILDING OF HOUSES.

HOWEVER, SOME WOMEN HAD BEEN KEEPING TRACK OF HOUSING MONEY USED IN PREVIOUS DEVELOPMENT PHASES OF CROSSROADS AND CAME FORWARD TO SUGGEST THAT THE RDP SUBSIDY BE INCREASED BY USING DEVELOP-MENT MONEY LEFT OVER FROM PREVIOUS BUILDING IN UNATHI, OR FROM MONEY DONATED TO CROSSROADS OVER THE YEARS.

THERE WERE MANY SERIOUS QUESTIONS RAISED BY MANY PEOPLE IN CROSSROADS AS TO THE DEMOCRATIC CREDENTIALS OF THE RDP FORUM, WHICH WAS THE INTERFACE BETWEEN SUBSIDIZED HOUSING PROCESSES AND PRODUCTS.

THE FORUM WAS MEANT TO ENSURE LOCAL PARTICIPATION IN ALL ASPECTS OF HOUSING AND ASSUMED TO BE THE MECHANISM TO RELAY CONCERNS AND CRITIQUES BETWEEN PEOPLE AND HIGHER LEVELS OF GOVERNMENT.

BUILDING OF ONE-ROOMED, BOUND-TO-CRACK HOUSES WERE SET TO CONTINUE IN JANUARY 1998.

WOMEN KNEW THAT DESPITE GOVERNMENT ATTEMPTS TO STANDARDIZE SUBSIDY HOUSING, THE FUNDING AND SIZE OPTIONS WERE NOT SET IN STONE, AND THAT THIS WAS THE TIME TO INTERVENE.

THE 1994 GOVERNMENT WHITE PAPER ON THE RDP ITSELF STATED THAT DEMOCRACY SHOULD NOT BE 'CONFINED TO PERIODIC ELECTIONS. IT IS, RATHER, AN ACTIVE PROCESS ENABLING EVERYONE TO CONTRIBUTE TO RECONSTRUCTION AND DEVELOPMENT.'

WOMEN IN CROSSROADS WERE KEENLY AWARE OF THE DANGERS INVOLVED IN INTERFERING IN HOUSING POLITICS. THEY HAD LIVED THROUGH DECADES OF ALLOCATION VIOLENCE AND FULLY GRASPED THE POTENTIAL REPERCUSSIONS OF 'DOING THE MATH.' THEY ORGANIZED STRATEGICALLY, ALONG GENDER LINES, FORMING A WOMEN-ONLY PROTEST GROUP, BYPASSING THE PARTY POLITICS THAT HAD COME TO BE ASSOCIATED WITH POLITICAL VIOLENCE IN CROSSROADS.

MAMA NGOZI, DESCRIBING HOW WOMEN'S POWER LAY IN THEIR GENDERED AND GENERATIONAL POSITIONS AS FOILS TO MALE AGGRESSION AND YOUTH IMPATIENCE:

UNLIKE MEN, WOMEN ARE SLOW TO ANGER AND THEY DON'T RUSH INTO FIGHTS.

THE WPG ORGANIZED WITHOUT MEN BECAUSE IN THEIR VIEW MEN WERE QUICK TO PULL THE TRIGGER WHEN THEY FELT THEIR POSITIONS THREATENED BY OTHER MEN.

THIS STRATEGY WAS NOT BASED ON OVERSIMPLIFIED POLITICAL ANALYSIS OF THE MEN-ARE-VIOLENT AND WOMEN-ARE-PEACEFUL VARIETY, BUT RATHER WAS ROOTED IN THEIR FRAMING OF WOMEN'S PARTICULAR CONCERNS.

THEY WERE SPEAKING TO THE ENDURING NEGLECT OF THE STATE AND TO POLITICAL VIOLENCE THAT SURROUNDED HOUSING POLITICS IN THE RECENT PAST.

WHILE SOME WOMEN WHO JOINED THE WPG HAD BEEN POLITICALLY ACTIVE IN THE 1970S, FOR THE MOST PART THESE WERE NOT IMFUDUSO WOMEN. THEY WERE WOMEN WHO HAD BEEN EXCLUDED FROM THE NEW CROSSROADS OPTION.

THEY HAD LIVED THROUGH NGXOBONGWANA, LOW-INTENSITY CONFLICT, AND THE POST-WITDOEKE CIVIL WAR OF OLD CROSSROADS.

THEY WERE WOMEN WHO MOSTLY BECAME POLITICALLY ACTIVE NOT IN THE 1970S BUT DURING THE EARLY 1990S, AND FOR THE MOST PART ATTEMPTED TO WORK THROUGH SQUATTER CIVICS LIKE WECUSA AND OFFICIAL PARTIES LIKE THE ANC AND PAC AND THEIR WOMEN AND YOUTH WINGS LIKE ANC WOMEN'S LEAGUE (ANCWL) AND AZANIA PEOPLE'S LIBERATION ARMY (APLA).

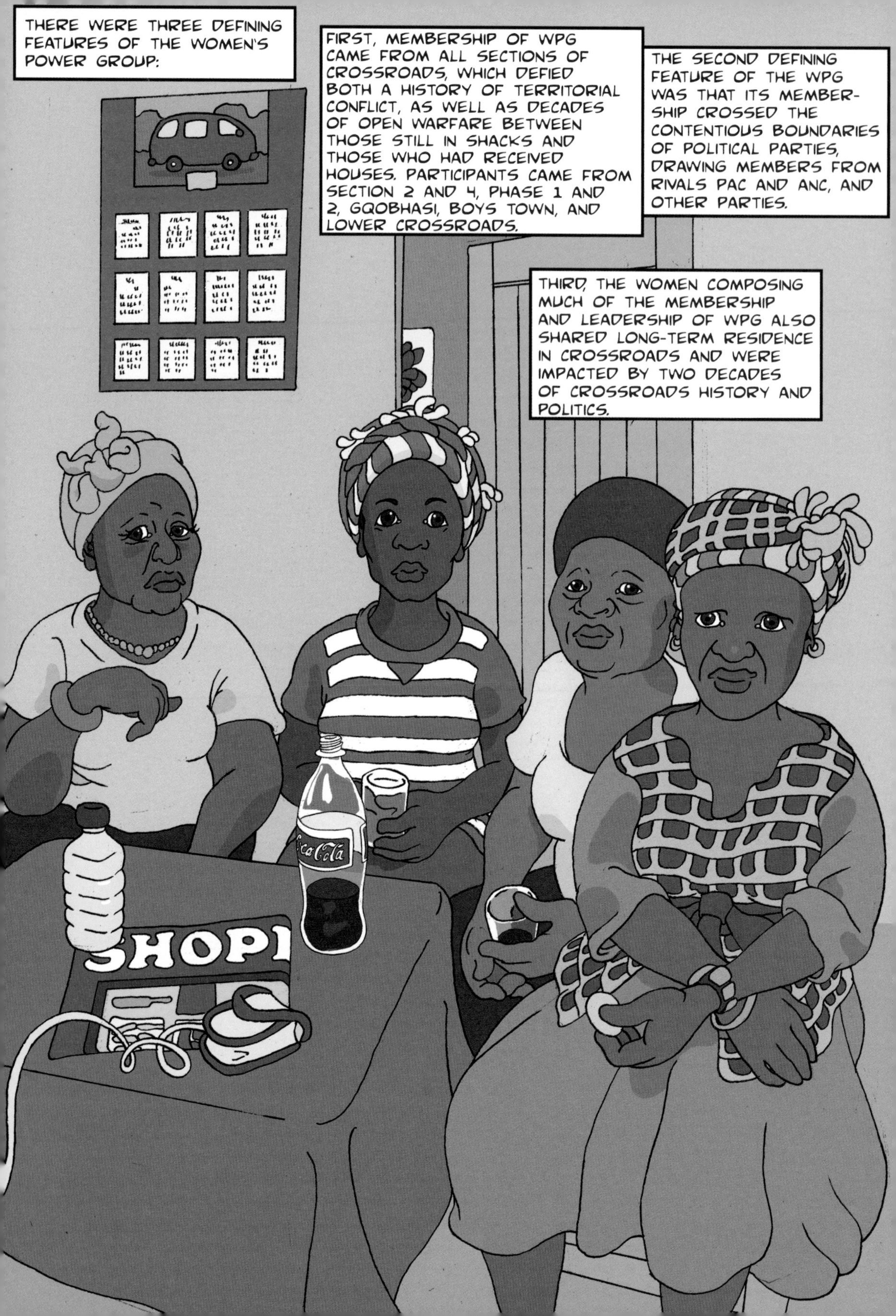

THERE WERE THREE DEFINING FEATURES OF THE WOMEN'S POWER GROUP:
FIRST, MEMBERSHIP OF WPG CAME FROM ALL SECTIONS OF CROSSROADS, WHICH DEFIED BOTH A HISTORY OF TERRITORIAL CONFLICT, AS WELL AS DECADES OF OPEN WARFARE BETWEEN THOSE STILL IN SHACKS AND THOSE WHO HAD RECEIVED HOUSES. PARTICIPANTS CAME FROM SECTION 2 AND 4, PHASE 1 AND 2, GQOBHASI, BOYS TOWN, AND LOWER CROSSROADS.
THE SECOND DEFINING FEATURE OF THE WPG WAS THAT ITS MEMBERSHIP CROSSED THE CONTENTIOUS BOUNDARIES OF POLITICAL PARTIES, DRAWING MEMBERS FROM RIVALS PAC AND ANC, AND OTHER PARTIES.
THIRD, THE WOMEN COMPOSING MUCH OF THE MEMBERSHIP AND LEADERSHIP OF WPG ALSO SHARED LONG-TERM RESIDENCE IN CROSSROADS AND WERE IMPACTED BY TWO DECADES OF CROSSROADS HISTORY AND POLITICS.
Coca-Cola
SHOPI

THE MAJORITY OF THE WPG WOMEN SEEMED TO BE WOMEN WHO HAD NOT BEEN PREVIOUSLY POLITICALLY ACTIVE BUT WHO HAD LIVED THROUGH ONE FORCED REMOVAL TOO MANY, AS MAMA MWANDA TIKA'S NARRATIVE SUGGESTS.

I CAME TO CAPE TOWN FROM TRANSKEI IN 1974. I WAS 27 YEARS OLD. MY HUSBAND HAD WORK BUT NO ACCOMMODATION, SO WE DECIDED TO BUILD A SHACK IN UNIBELL.

'AFTER OUR SHACK WAS DESTROYED IN THE UNIBELL CAMP DEMOLITIONS BY THE APARTHEID GOVERNMENT WE MOVED TO THE 'CROSSROADS FOREST.'

'NGXOBONGWANA HELPED ME TO GET A PASS. HE TOLD ME, "YOU DON'T HAVE TO GO ANYWHERE, YOU WERE BORN HERE IN SOUTH AFRICA."'

'OUR SHACK WAS BURNT DOWN AGAIN BY "THE COMRADES" IN 1986. THEY SAID THAT ANYONE WHO DON'T SUPPORT THEM ARE SELL-OUTS.'

'WE RETURNED WHEN NGXOBONGWANA SAID THAT WE SHOULD COME BACK TO CROSSROADS. WE REBUILT OUR SHACK, NO. 932, AT MPUME-LELWENI, SECTION 3.'

'THEN OUR HOUSE WAS BURNT DOWN AGAIN, IN 1990, WHEN NONGWE WAS FIGHTING MGEBE.'

'THE SHACK I AM LIVING IN NOW I BOUGHT IN 1993, FROM MRS. SOGA, WHO MOVED TO KHAYELITSHA AFTER HER HUSBAND WAS SHOT DURING THE FORCED REMOVALS TO LOWER CROSSROADS.'

ADDRESS THE COUNCIL MEMBERS DEEMED RESPONSIBLE FOR THEIR CONCERNS BY NOMINATING REPRESENTATIVES TO SPEAK TO COUNCILLORS INDIVIDUALLY.

MASS ACTION, ACCORDING TO MAMA SHUGU, WAS INITIALLY AVOIDED BECAUSE IT WAS ASSOCIATED WITH PRISON THAT LEFT UNATTENDED SHACKS VULNERABLE TO ARSON.

THUS THEY APPROACHED COUNCILLOR GWAYI.

ACCORDING TO THE PRESS, MR. GWAYI SAID THAT WHEN THE WOMEN'S GROUP WAS FORMED THEY DEMANDED TO KNOW FROM HIM WHAT HAD HAPPENED TO R35 MILLION SET ASIDE BY THE FORMER IKAPA TOWN COUNCIL FOR THE UPGRADE OF THE AREA. THE WOMEN ALSO DEMANDED THAT THE CONSTRUCTION OF THE HOUSES BE STOPPED BECAUSE THEY WERE TOO SMALL.

WHEN NOT IGNORED, WPG MEMBERS WERE PASSED FROM ONE DEPARTMENT AND LEVEL OF GOVERNMENT TO ANOTHER; NEITHER COUNCILLOR GWAYI NOR NCATE FOLLOWED THROUGH ON THEIR ASSURANCES THAT THEY WOULD TAKE THE WOMEN'S ISSUES FORWARD AND REPORT BACK RESPONSES. THE THIRD CROSSROADS COUNCILLOR, ELESE DEPOUTCH, HAD REFUSED TO MEET AT ALL.

AS THE WOMEN ATTEMPTED TO MEET WITH COUNCILLORS, THE GROUP GREW.

AT THE END OF NOVEMBER 1997, WPG APPROACHED A LONGSTANDING NGO WORKER IN THE AREA WHO ARRANGED A SET OF MEETINGS FOR JANUARY 1998.

TWICE THESE MEETINGS WERE SUSPENDED WHEN COUNCILLORS REFUSED TO ATTEND AND HAD THE COMMUNITY HALL LOCKED.

FRUSTRATED, THE WPG DECIDED TO GO AND SIT AT THE COUNCIL OFFICES UNTIL THEY RECEIVED SOME SATISFACTORY RESPONSE.

THUS BEGAN THE WPG SIT-IN ON JANUARY 21, 1998.

A CONSISTENT CORE OF ABOUT 10 WOMEN COORDINATED THE SIT-IN WITH A ROTATING SCHEDULE, SO THAT AT ANY ONE TIME THERE WOULD BE UP TO 50 WOMEN SITTING AT THE ADMINISTRATION OFFICE.

THE OCCUPATION CAUGHT THE ATTENTION OF THE ANC WHO IMMEDIATELY HELD AN EXECUTIVE MEETING TO QUESTION COUNCILLOR ELESE DEPOUTCH ABOUT WPG ALLEGATIONS. THE ANC EXECUTIVE DECIDED THAT 'THE WOMEN WHO WERE MEMBERS OF THE ANC SHOULD EXCUSE THEMSELVES FROM THE WPG.'

ON JANUARY 25 ELESE DEPOUTCH MET WITH THE WOMEN WHERE HE DECLARED ALL ALLEGATIONS AGAINST HIM INVALID.

THREE DAYS LATER THE ANC CHAIR OF THE WESTERN CAPE AND THE ANC WOMEN'S LEAGUE REPRESENTATIVE WENT TO 'TALK TO THE WOMEN.' THE ANC THEN WENT AND OFFICIALLY TOLD THE ANC WOMEN TO STEP DOWN.

IT TOOK THE CITY COUNCIL SOME TWO WEEKS TO REALIZE THAT THE WOMEN WERE SERIOUS ABOUT GETTING ANSWERS.

ON FEBRUARY 2 COUNCILLORS GWAYI AND DEPOUTCH APPROACHED THE SIT-IN AND HEARD COMPLAINTS.

ON FEBRUARY 3 PATRICK MAKHURA, THE EXECUTIVE COMMITTEE SUPPORT OFFICER IN CHARGE OF EXPLAINING NEW SERVICE FEES, WAS CALLED IN BECAUSE A GROUP OF APPROXIMATELY 20 WOMEN HAD OCCUPIED THE CROSSROADS ADMIN OFFICES ASKING FOR CLARITY ON THE INTERIM COMMUNITY SERVICE CHARGES.

AFTER HIS 20-MINUTE PRESENTATION HE RECALLED THAT MRS. MBEKA THANKED HIM AND SAID THAT THE WOMEN WERE CLEARER ON THE POSITION, BUT THEY HAD ALSO COME TO FIND OUT WHAT HAPPENED TO THE FUNDING DONATED TO THE CROSSROADS COMMUNITY.

REPORTS BY MRS. MBEKA SHOWED NO CONFUSION OVER SERVICE FEE INCREASES, BUT RATHER AN OUTRIGHT REJECTION OF MAKHURA'S RESPONSE.

THE WPG THEN PRESENTED MAKHURA WITH THEIR DEMANDS, WHICH INCLUDED: 48 SQ. METER HOUSES; THE WHERE-ABOUTS OF DEVELOPMENT FUNDING; ANSWERS AS TO WHY RATES HAD INCREASED FOR SITES NOT SERVICED; AND TO SPEAK TO THE MAYOR.

AS PROMISED, MAKHURA REPORTED TO THE HEAD OF THE EXECUTIVE COMMITTEE, NOMAINDA MFEKETO AND CALLED A MEETING WITH COUNCILLORS DEPOUTCH AND GWAYI, WHO TOLD HIM THAT THE WPG SIT-IN WAS A POLITICAL PLOY BY OPPOSITION.

ON FEBRUARY 5 MAYOR TERESA SOLOMON AND EXCO'S MFEKETO, BOTH OF WHOM WERE CRUCIALLY INVOLVED IN THE LIBERATION STRUGGLE AS FEMINIST POLITICAL ACTIVISTS, ADDRESSED THE WOMEN. WHEN THE WPG WENT TO FOLLOW UP WITH THE MAYOR ON FEBRUARY 9 SHE WAS UNAVAILABLE.

THE TEN WPG REPRESENTATIVES WERE INSTEAD SEEN BY ANDREW BORAINE AND PATRICK MAKHURA.

AT THIS MEETING WOMEN ELABORATED ON ISSUES OF HEALTH, CONSTRUCTION, REPRESENTATION AND LACK OF SERVICE DELIVERY.

BY FEBRUARY 9 THE CITY HAD CATEGORIZED THE WOMEN'S CONCERNS INTO 'POLITICAL ISSUES' (WHICH WERE SAID TO BE BEYOND THE COUNCIL'S JURISDICTION), AS WELL AS FINANCE, COMMUNITY AND ENGINEERING SERVICES – 'EACH AND EVERYONE OF WHICH,' COUNCIL ARGUED, 'HAD BEEN RESOLVED.'

COUNCIL THUS REQUESTED THAT THE WOMEN'S REPRESENTATIVES REPORT BACK TO THE REST OF THE GROUP AND VACATE THE CITY COUNCIL OFFICES.

ON FEBRUARY 12 MRS. CHUKU, OF THE WPG, PHONED MAKHURA TO SAY THAT THE WOMEN WOULD NOT MOVE UNTIL THEIR 'POLITICAL DEMANDS' AS THEY WERE NOW CALLED, WERE MET.

CONSEQUENTLY THE CITY COUNCIL DECIDED TO USE THE POLICE AND COURTS TO EVICT THE WOMEN.

INDIVIDUAL ARRESTS AND CHARGES FOR TRESPASSING BEGAN ON FRIDAY THE 12TH. WOMEN WERE 'PEACEFULLY EVICTED' BY POLICE — THE WPG STRATEGY AT THIS POINT WAS TO COOPERATE WITH POLICE AND REPLACE ARRESTED MEMBERS.

THE RESULTS OF THE ARRESTS WERE THREEFOLD:

—FIRST, THEY BROUGHT MEDIA ATTENTION WHICH IN TURN CAST A SPOTLIGHT ON THE ISSUES OF THE WPG.

—SECOND, THEY INCREASED WOMEN'S DEMANDS AND METHODS OF PROTEST. INSTEAD OF WAITING FOR THE COUNCILLORS' RESPONSE, THEY WERE NOW WAITING FOR THEIR DEMANDS TO BE MET.

AT THIS POINT SOME WOMEN, LIKE MAMA ELSIE MKHUMBUZI, FELT THE WPG HAD LOST ITS FOCUS. WHILE THEY HAD STARTED OUT FIGHTING AGAINST 'MATCHBOX-SIZED' HOUSES, NOW THEY WERE 'JUST OPPOSING EVERYTHING THE GOVERNMENT IS PUTTING ON THE TABLE.'

WHILE THE WPG LOST SOME MEMBERS AS ITS STANCE HARDENED, IT CERTAINLY GAINED OTHERS, WITH OVER 300 WOMEN OCCUPYING THE ADMINISTRATION OFFICES AT ITS PEAK.

HENCE THE THIRD SHIFT MARKED BY THE ARRESTS WAS THE WIDESPREAD AND DIVERSELY MOTIVATED 'SUPPORT,' WHICH INCREASED TENSIONS IN CROSSROADS AS IT BROUGHT IN THE TYPE OF POLITICAL VIOLENCE THAT THE WPG HAD SET OUT TO AVOID.

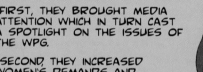

MAMA ELSIE MKHUMBUZI

THE CITY'S TURN AWAY FROM ADDRESSING THE CONCERNS OF THE WPG TO THE USE OF FORCE TO REMOVE THE WOMEN MARKED THE FIRST AND UNFORTUNATELY NOT THE THE LAST INCREASE IN INTENSITY OF THE SIT-IN.

DURING MARCH AND APRIL THE SIT-IN BEGAN TO SPREAD BEYOND THE ADMINISTRATION OFFICES TO THE GROUNDS SURROUNDING THE BUILDING AND THEN INTO THE REST OF CROSSROADS.

WITHIN THE ADMINISTRATION OFFICES AGGRESSION ROSE AS WORK WAS DISRUPTED, WORKERS WERE APPARENTLY BEATEN AND SERVICE MONIES WERE LEFT UNPAID.

AS FRUSTRATION TURNED TO AGGRESSION AND 'SUPPORT' BEGAN TO BUILD, THE WOMEN, AS AN ORGANIZED GROUP, SLOWLY LOST CONTROL OF THE PROTEST BEYOND THE BUILDING.

THE SIT-IN, HOWEVER, REMAINED A WOMEN'S INITIATIVE AND SPACE.

WHILE MEN HELPED THEM TO GET BACK INTO THE BUILDING AND WERE OUTSIDE 'PROTECTING' THE WOMEN, THEY DID NOT JOIN THE OCCUPATION.

IN MARCH BOTH THE WPG AND THE COUNCILLORS STILL ATTEMPTED TO RALLY SUPPORT FOR WHAT HAD BECOME TWO 'SIDES' OF CONTESTATION.

COUNCILLOR DEPOUTCH ORGANIZED MASS MEETINGS AND THE MASAKHANE MARCH ON THE ADMINISTRATION BUILDINGS TO ENCOURAGE RESIDENTS TO PAY SERVICE FEES.

HE ALSO HIRED A SECOND BUILDING CONTRACTOR TO HELP SPEED UP THE BUILDING OF HOUSES IN CROSSROADS.

THE WPG ALSO STAGED A MARCH TO PARLIAMENT TO VOICE THEIR CONCERNS AND APPEALED TO THE PROVINCE, WHOSE MINISTER FOR LOCAL GOVERNMENT, PATRICK MCKENZIE, WAS QUOTED IN THE NEWSPAPER SAYING THAT HE WOULD 'INSTRUCT THE IKAPA COUNCIL TO SUSPEND BUILDING HOUSES, WHICH RESIDENTS CLAIM ARE TOO SMALL, IN OLD CROSSROADS' AND HE WOULD COMMUNICATE WITH THE POLICE TO STOP HARASSING THE WOMEN AND EVICTING THEM FROM THE COUNCIL PREMISES.

IN RESPONSE THE CITY COUNCIL COMPLAINED TO THE PREMIER OF THE WESTERN CAPE (HERNUS KRIEL) THAT HIS MINISTER, PATRICK MCKENZIE, HAD ACTED IN 'BAD FAITH' AND HAD INTERFERED IN LOCAL GOVERNMENT.

ON APRIL 15 THE S.A. POLICE RECEIVED INSTRUCTION FROM THE PUBLIC PROSECUTOR THAT THE WPG WOMEN COULD BE ARRESTED AND PROSECUTED.

THE FOLLOWING DAY SIX WOMEN WERE DETAINED AND THE REST OF THE WOMEN WERE FORCED OUT OF THE COMPLEX, ONLY TO PUSH BACK THROUGH THE GATES AND 'SIT' INSIDE THE GATES.

ARRESTS WERE PERCEIVED TO BE AD HOC, 'WHOEVER RAN FAST GOT AWAY.'

THE MITCHELL'S PLAIN MAGISTRATE'S COURT ISSUED AN INTERDICT RESTRAINING THE WPG MEMBERS FROM INTERFERING WITH THE DEVELOPMENT PROGRAM.

THE CROSSROADS COMMUNITY POLICE FORUM DESCRIBED THE INTENSIFICATION OF SHACK BURNINGS AND SHOOTINGS WHICH THEY SAID RESULTED FROM WPG MEMBERS BLOCKADING CONTRACTORS ON APRIL 16 AND 17, 1998.

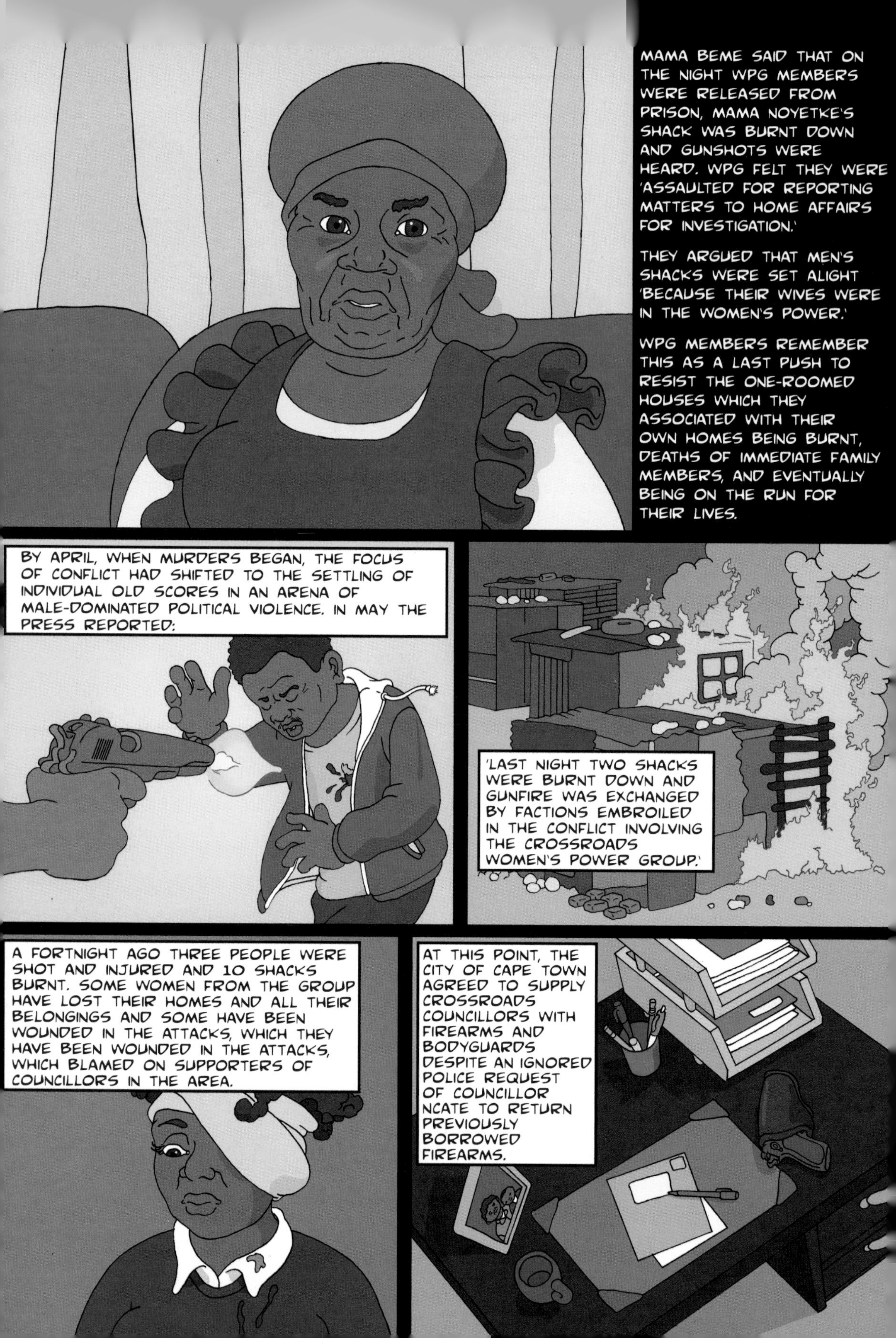
MAMA BEME SAID THAT ON THE NIGHT WPG MEMBERS WERE RELEASED FROM PRISON, MAMA NOYETKE'S SHACK WAS BURNT DOWN AND GUNSHOTS WERE HEARD. WPG FELT THEY WERE 'ASSAULTED FOR REPORTING MATTERS TO HOME AFFAIRS FOR INVESTIGATION.'
THEY ARGUED THAT MEN'S SHACKS WERE SET ALIGHT 'BECAUSE THEIR WIVES WERE IN THE WOMEN'S POWER.'
WPG MEMBERS REMEMBER THIS AS A LAST PUSH TO RESIST THE ONE-ROOMED HOUSES WHICH THEY ASSOCIATED WITH THEIR OWN HOMES BEING BURNT, DEATHS OF IMMEDIATE FAMILY MEMBERS, AND EVENTUALLY BEING ON THE RUN FOR THEIR LIVES.
BY APRIL, WHEN MURDERS BEGAN, THE FOCUS OF CONFLICT HAD SHIFTED TO THE SETTLING OF INDIVIDUAL OLD SCORES IN AN ARENA OF MALE-DOMINATED POLITICAL VIOLENCE. IN MAY THE PRESS REPORTED:
'LAST NIGHT TWO SHACKS WERE BURNT DOWN AND GUNFIRE WAS EXCHANGED BY FACTIONS EMBROILED IN THE CONFLICT INVOLVING THE CROSSROADS WOMEN'S POWER GROUP.'
A FORTNIGHT AGO THREE PEOPLE WERE SHOT AND INJURED AND 10 SHACKS BURNT. SOME WOMEN FROM THE GROUP HAVE LOST THEIR HOMES AND ALL THEIR BELONGINGS AND SOME HAVE BEEN WOUNDED IN THE ATTACKS, WHICH THEY HAVE BEEN WOUNDED IN THE ATTACKS, WHICH BLAMED ON SUPPORTERS OF COUNCILLORS IN THE AREA.
AT THIS POINT, THE CITY OF CAPE TOWN AGREED TO SUPPLY CROSSROADS COUNCILLORS WITH FIREARMS AND BODYGUARDS DESPITE AN IGNORED POLICE REQUEST OF COUNCILLOR NCATE TO RETURN PREVIOUSLY BORROWED FIREARMS.

SUBSEQUENTLY THE CITY COUNCIL ALSO SUPPLIED THE CROSSROADS COUNCILLORS WITH BAIL MONEY WHEN CHARGED WITH MURDER, WHICH WAS ALSO A PRACTICE OFFICIALLY BEING CONDEMNED BY THE ANC.

BY MAY, 10 PEOPLE HAD DIED AND AT LEAST 40 FAMILIES (200-400) HAD LOST THEIR HOMES.

THE POLICE APPROACHED AN NGO, U-MAN AGING CONFLICT TO INTERVENE, STATING THAT THEY WERE SCARED TO STEP IN.

THUS A COMMUNITY POLICING FORUM WAS ESTABLISHED TO TRY AND ADDRESS THE VIOLENCE.

ON APRIL 17, MR. STULO AND MR. SIDINANA WERE ATTACKED. SIDINANA, ACCORDING TO THE PAC, HAD BEEN THREATENING THE HOUSES AND LIVES OF THE WPG.

A WEEK LATER, STULO WAS MURDERED AND ATTEMPTS WERE MADE ON DEPOUTCH'S LIFE.

AS CHAIR OF THE RDP, STULO'S MURDER COULD BE SEEN AS A WPG STANCE AGAINST IMPOSED DEVELOPMENT.

WPG MEMBERS WERE VAGUE ON THE MATTER:

NO ONE KNOWS WHO KILLED HIM BECAUSE OUR CHILDREN AND BROTHERS HELPED US WHEN WE WERE ATTACKED.

DEPOUTCH DID NOT BLAME THE WPG FOR ATTACKS ON HIS LIFE.

YET THEY WERE STILL IMPLICATED BECAUSE ONE OF THE ARMED PAC YOUTH ATTACKERS ACCUSED BY DEPOUTCH WAS THEMBELANI NGOZI, SON AND PARTNER OF TWO LEADING WPG MEMBERS WHO WAS THEN SHOT DEAD ON MAY 9, 1998.

TO THE WPG, TARGETED SHOOTINGS THAT RESULTED IN THEMBELANI'S DEATH SYMBOLIZED THE WAY THEIR SIT-IN WAS INVERTED FROM AN ATTEMPT TO DRAW ATTENTION TO ISSUES OF HOUSING AND DEVELOPMENT INTO A PLAYING FIELD USED TO SETTLE OLD SCORES.

THEMBELANI'S FUNERAL WAS ON MAY 30.

AT THE FUNERAL, HIS GRANDMOTHER, MAMA NGOZI'S MOTHER, WAS STABBED TO DEATH AND TWO OTHERS WERE INJURED

TENSIONS ROSE ON THE DAY OF THE FUNERAL AS ELESE DEPOUTCH, WHO LIVED NEXT DOOR TO THE NGOZI'S IN UNATHI, WAS SEEN SLAUGHTER-ING A GOAT, WHICH, TO THE WPG, SYMBOLIZED HIS CELEBRATION OF THEMBELANI'S DEATH.

COUNCILLOR DEPOUTCH CLAIMED THAT THIS WAS PURELY COINCIDENTAL, AS HE WAS PREPARING FOR THE LAUNCH OF THE ANC YOUTH LEAGUE.

THE ATTACK ON THE FUNERAL TRIGGERED A SLEW OF COUNTER-ATTACKS AND REVENGE KILLINGS.

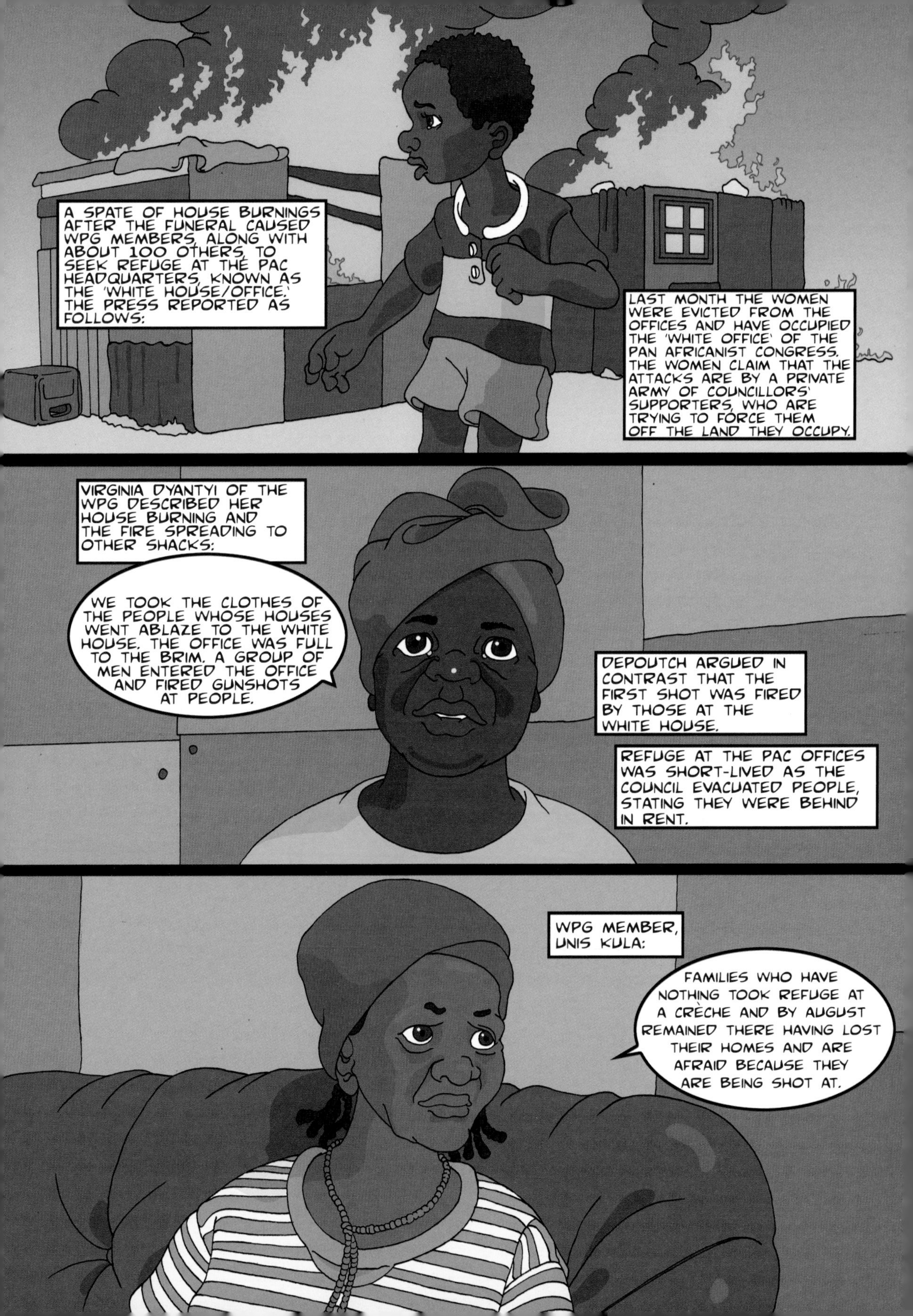
A SPATE OF HOUSE BURNINGS AFTER THE FUNERAL CAUSED WPG MEMBERS, ALONG WITH ABOUT 100 OTHERS, TO SEEK REFUGE AT THE PAC HEADQUARTERS, KNOWN AS THE 'WHITE HOUSE/OFFICE.' THE PRESS REPORTED AS FOLLOWS:
LAST MONTH THE WOMEN WERE EVICTED FROM THE OFFICES AND HAVE OCCUPIED THE 'WHITE OFFICE' OF THE PAN AFRICANIST CONGRESS. THE WOMEN CLAIM THAT THE ATTACKS ARE BY A PRIVATE ARMY OF COUNCILLORS' SUPPORTERS, WHO ARE TRYING TO FORCE THEM OFF THE LAND THEY OCCUPY.
VIRGINIA DYANTYI OF THE WPG DESCRIBED HER HOUSE BURNING AND THE FIRE SPREADING TO OTHER SHACKS:
WE TOOK THE CLOTHES OF THE PEOPLE WHOSE HOUSES WENT ABLAZE TO THE WHITE HOUSE. THE OFFICE WAS FULL TO THE BRIM. A GROUP OF MEN ENTERED THE OFFICE AND FIRED GUNSHOTS AT PEOPLE.
DEPOUTCH ARGUED IN CONTRAST THAT THE FIRST SHOT WAS FIRED BY THOSE AT THE WHITE HOUSE.
REFUGE AT THE PAC OFFICES WAS SHORT-LIVED AS THE COUNCIL EVACUATED PEOPLE, STATING THEY WERE BEHIND IN RENT.
WPG MEMBER, UNIS KULA:
FAMILIES WHO HAVE NOTHING TOOK REFUGE AT A CRÈCHE AND BY AUGUST REMAINED THERE HAVING LOST THEIR HOMES AND ARE AFRAID BECAUSE THEY ARE BEING SHOT AT.

THE PRESS REPORTED A MONTH OF ABSENTEEISM AT SCHOOLS:

'CHILDREN OF MEMBERS OF WOMEN'S POWER HAVE HAD THEIR LIVES THREATENED AND ARE AFRAID TO ATTEND SCHOOL.'

CROSSROADS-WIDE POLICE RAIDS CONTINUED.

VIRGINIA DYANTYI: 'THE DAY AFTER THE FUNERAL ATTACKS, THE POLICE BROKE DOWN DOORS OF HOUSES LOOKING FOR GUNS, AND THE NEXT DAY FIVE TAXIS ARRIVED AND STARTED SHOOTING INDISCRIMINATELY.'

QUEEN SHUGU

SOME PEOPLE RAN AWAY FROM CROSSROADS. I REMEMBER RUNNING AWAY FOR SAFETY AND LEAVING MY CHILDREN HERE...

MRS. NGOZI, MRS. STYODANA, AND I RAN FOR SAFETY...I ESCAPED FROM THE 1ST OF JULY TILL THE 1ST OF NOVEMBER, I CAME BACK.

SOME LEFT LITERALLY RUNNING AND OTHERS WEIGHED UP THE DECISION FOR SOME TIME. MRS. MKHEFA, A WPG LEADER, HAD BEEN THREATENED AND ASKED TO LEAVE CROSSROADS. SHE SAID THAT THE POLICE DIRECTOR, MPEMBE, ADVISED HER TO GO IF SHE DID NOT HAVE THE SAME SHOOTING POWER AS THOSE THREATENING HER.

ON THE DAY THAT SOTASHE NOMANA WAS KILLED IN UNATHI, MKHEFA WAS SHOT AT BY TWO MEN. AFTER SHE LEFT THE AREA, HER BELONGINGS WERE STOLEN.

MOUNTING TENSION, ARSON ATTACKS, AND SEVERAL FATAL SHOOTINGS CONTINUED INTO JUNE AND JULY.

DURING THIS TIME NONGWE WAS PERMANENTLY CHASED OUT OF CROSSROADS BY YOUTH FROM SECTION 4, MAMA LUKE'S HOUSE WAS BURNT TO THE GROUND, AND SHUGU'S SISTER WAS KILLED.

ON JULY 21 MORE THAN 20 SHACKS, INCLUDING A HOUSE OF COUNCILLOR GWAYI, WERE SET ALIGHT.

MAMA HAMSA'S CRÈCHE WAS BURNT TO THE GROUND.

WHILE DEPOUTCH CLAIMED THAT IN OCTOBER THE WPG WERE 'STILL IN EVIDENCE' AND NONGWE AND NGXOBONGWANA HAD BEEN SEEN IN CROSSROADS, THE WPG HAD, BY DECEMBER, BEEN DISBANDED, THEIR ORGANIZING HAVING BEEN KILLED OFF BY OCTOBER.

AS A GROUP THE WPG MADE THEIR LAST STAND IN THE REFUSAL TO VACATE THE LAST 13 REMAINING SHACKS THAT IMPEDED HOUSING DEVELOPMENT IN PHASE 3. BETWEEN MARCH AND JULY WPG HAD BEEN CHASED AWAY FROM THE DEVELOPMENT SITE BUT THEY REFUSED TO TAKE DOWN THEIR SHACKS.

FOR PHASE 3 DEVELOPMENT THE ENTIRE COMMUNITY OF SECTION 2 HAD BEEN RELOCATED TO A SCHOOL SITE IN PHASE 4. OBSTRUCTION OF THE COMPLETION OF PHASE 3 WAS COSTLY. NEGOTIATIONS HAD PROVEN UNSUCCESSFUL AND THE PROVINCIAL AUTHORITY WAS RELUCTANT TO INITIATE YET ANOTHER DRAWN OUT REQUEST FOR A COURT ORDER.

NO COURT ORDER WAS EVER OBTAINED AND THE OFFICIAL COMMISSION INTO THE CROSSROADS CRISIS REPRIMANDED ELESE DEPOUTCH FOR ILLEGALLY AND PERSONALLY DEMOLISHING THOSE SHACKS WITH THE USE OF HIS OWN SECURITY PERSONNEL IN SEPTEMBER.

IN JUNE THE PRESS ANNOUNCED THAT THE CAPE TOWN MUNICIPALITY WAS LAUNCHING AN URGENT INVESTIGATION INTO CONFLICT IN OLD CROSSROADS. THE FOCUS OF THE INVESTIGATION HAD SHIFTED FROM LOOKING INTO THE WPG'S 'BACKGROUND, MEMBERSHIP AND BEGINNINGS,' SUGGESTED BY ELESE DEPOUTCH IN MARCH TO FOCUSING ON THE VIOLENCE, PARTY POLITICS AND THE MEN WITH GUNS.'

THIS SHIFT DISHEARTENED MANY WOULD-BE WPG SUPPORTERS.

THE HOUSING DEPARTMENT TERMINATED THE DISPUTED CONTRACT, AGREEING WITH THE WOMEN THAT IT WAS IMPOSSIBLE TO BUILD BIGGER HOUSES WITH THIS SUBSIDY.

HOWEVER, INHERENT IN THIS 'WIN' WAS ALSO THE RELE-GITIMIZATION OF THE COUN-CILLORS IN CROSSROADS WHOM THE WOMEN FELT WERE A HINDRANCE TO DEMOCRATIC PARTICIPATION.

THE OLD CONTRACTS WERE CANCELLED BUT NO ALTERNATIVE HOUSING PROPOSALS WERE FORTHCOMING.

THE PROJECT WAS SOON RESTARTED WITH FEW CHANGES MADE TO THE ORIGINAL PLANS.

BY AUGUST PEOPLE WERE MOVING INTO THE NEW, ONE-ROOMED HOUSES, BUT THE CONFLICT CONTINUED.

FOLLOWING THE SIT-IN THE WPG'S ACTIONS WERE IMMEDIATELY RESCRIPTED INTO AN OFFICIAL ACCOUNT OF POLITICAL DIVISIONS AND TENSIONS: AN ALTERNATIVE NARRATIVE WHICH MISREPRESENTED THEIR CAMPAIGN AND WORKED TO UNDERMINE THEM FURTHER.

SUGGESTED IN MARCH, THE COMMISSION OF ENQUIRY WAS INITIALLY INTENDED TO FOCUS ON THE WPG, BUT BY THE TIME THE ENQUIRY TOOK PLACE IN JULY, ATTENTION WAS RE-CENTRED ON MALE LEADERSHIP BATTLES.

AFTER HEARING 39 TESTIMONIES (SEVEN OF WHICH WERE FROM THE WPG) THE COMMISSION'S ANALYSIS FOCUSED ON FIVE SOURCES OF WHAT IT DEEMED TO BE 'GENUINE VIOLENT RIVALRY' THAT HIGHLIGHTED MALE-DOMINATED LEADERSHIP TENSIONS.

WPG WOMEN WERE ASCRIBED TO POLITICAL CAMPS, REGARDLESS OF HOW THEIR ACTIONS AND THE EVIDENCE THEY GAVE TO THE COMMISSION BLATANTLY CONTRADICTED SUCH ASCRIPTION.

PARTY POLITICS WERE PRIORITIZED BY THE COMMISSION, WHICH INSISTED ON DEFINING THE WPG AS AN INTEREST GROUP ALLIED WITH THE PAC AGAINST THE COUNCILLORS/ ANC DESPITE AMPLE EVIDENCE TO THE CONTRARY.

PRIOR TO THE SIT-IN, THE WPG HAD APPROACHED AND BEEN REFUSED HELP BY ALL ORGANIZATIONS LISTED BY THE COMMISSION, FROM THE ANC TO THE PAC, TO THE WESTERN CAPE UNITED SQUATTERS ASSOCIATION (WECUSA).

THE WPG SIT-IN CAN BE SEEN AS A WINDOW INTO WHAT WOMEN'S ACTIVISM WAS UP AGAINST IN POST-APARTHEID CROSSROADS. THE RESPONSE TO THEIR ATTEMPTS TO POLITICIZE THEIR HOUSING STRUGGLES EXPOSE HOW THE NEGOTIATED TRANSITION FROM 'LOW-INTENSITY CONFLICT' TO 'LOW-INTENSITY DEMOCRACY' PLAYED OUT ACROSS THEIR LIVES.

THE SIT-IN BECAME PART OF A STRUGGLE TO MAINTAIN AND NORMALIZE DIVIDE-AND-RULE ASPECTS OF THE POLITICS OF ALLOCATING SCARCE RESOURCES.

THE INSISTENCE THAT 1994 WAS A MILESTONE, WHICH SIGNIFIED A BREAK FROM PAST SUFFERING, ALSO SERVED TO CHALLENGE THE LEGITIMACY OF THE WPG'S CONCERNS. LIKE THE APARTHEID STATE, THE POST-COLONIAL STATE HAS DEFENDED ITSELF AGAINST THE IMPERATIVE OF PROVIDING BASIC SOCIAL SERVICES BY PUSHING THIS RESPONSIBILITY BACK INTO THE PRIVATE HOUSEHOLD SPHERE, AND ON TO THE SHOULDERS OF AFRICAN WOMEN.

NOSISI MBEKA

A DECADE INTO DEMOCRACY, NOSISI MBEKA SPEAKS ABOUT ONGOING STRUGGLES FOR WOMEN IN CROSSROADS THAT CONTINUED AFTER THE WOMEN'S POWER GROUP:

'US PEOPLE IN BOYS TOWN, WE ARE STILL IN THE APARTHEID TIME.'

'I CAN'T SAY I'M IN TEN YEARS OF FREEDOM. I'M IN TEN YEARS OF STRUGGLE.'

Re:Sources

Many archives have been consulted and constructed in the process of putting this history together. These collections are spread far and wide and include materials such as newspaper clippings, audio and transcripts of interviews, photographic and video footage, slideshows, newsletters, pamphlets, commissions, testimonies, legal records, etc. Without getting in the way of telling the story of Crossroads women's organizing and the building of Cape Town, we have tried to pepper these sources in, sometimes explicitly indicating and sometimes subtly hinting at these sources throughout this book.

By far the most important archive has been people, as living archives, and the life narratives and oral histories produced with those involved in the organized movements of the struggles in and over Crossroads. Full citations of all the primary sources, including the interviews used to build this history are available in detail in the original thesis, listed as one of the published/secondary source texts in the bibliography below.

The Crossroads Women's Committee history is recollected through interviews with women and some men on the frontlines of this struggle, as well as with support workers involved in various ways at the time. This includes interviews with thirty-six key people involved including: Jane Yanta, Adelaide Mene, Nomangezi Muriel Mbobosi, Daisy Bara, Eslina Mapisa, Victoria Mkondweni, Mrs. Viki, Mrs. Msaba, Mrs. Sigwela, Mrs. Tshingana, Selena Dasi, Mrs. Ngozi, Mrs. Tomsana, Nomandla Tomsana, Elsie Mkhumbuzi, Selena Poswayo, Mama Poswayo, Siswe Yohane, Winnie Nkosi, Nozuko Peters, Mrs. Ndyalvane, Millicent Nongxa Ngxobongwana, Nomahobe Tom, Mrs. Dutoit Stuurman, Nontuthuzelo Jobela, Spokazi Luke, Gladys Nofemela, Oliver Memani, Sam Ndima, Mr. Mchobololo, Mr. Tomsana, Mr. Lutango, Josette Cole, Michael Richman, Francis Wilson, Dot Clemenshaw, It also includes testimonies given in government Commissions, and transcripts of interviews done by researchers, journalists, and activists in the 1970s, 1980s, and 1990s (including with Regina Ntongana who had passed on by 2005).

The Women's Power Group history is recollected through individual and group interviews with twenty-four women involved (Mamas Beme, Dasi, Kwinana, Kwana, Kontyolo, Xhapha, Mzikulu, Ngxiya, Mdyeshana, Mwanda-Tika, Mbeka, Totose, Nqimtza, Mkhumbuzi, Ngozi, Tomsana, Sogo-Hamse, Shugu, Mangqamba, Mgedzi, Tom, Jobela, Luke, Conjwa) and also three men (Noludwe, Ntwasa, Mfana), one councillor (Depoutch) and two non-governmental organisation (NGO) workers (Greenwell, Sopongisa). It also draws on press interviews from the time and the analysis and thirty-nine oral testimonies given to the 1998 Commission (including Mamas Kula, Dyantyi, Mbeka, key women leaders who had passed away by 2005).

Ten of the full transcripts from interviews (with Jane Yanta, Muriel Mbobosi, Adelaide Mene, Daisy Bara, Victoria Mkondweni, Selena Dasi, Weziwe Sogo-Hamse, Queen Shugu Tynto, Sylvia Ngozi, and Sam Ndima) are available in full on the Aluka Digitalization of Southern African Liberation Struggles website: https://www.aluka.org/stable/10.5555/al.sff.document. ae000011.

The bibliography included here is a partial list of published research that contributed to this book. These are histories of land dispossession, forced removals, organized resistance, social movements, urbanization, the negotiated settlement, and studies on housing, politics, gender and militarization, and memory. It also includes some writing on feminist collaborative research practices, radical education experiments, critical approaches to archives, and some of the inspirational graphic histories that sparked this book.

Bibliography

Abrahams, Yvette. "Images of Sara Bartman: Sexuality, Race and Gender in Early-Nineteenth-Century Britain." In *Nation, Empire, Colony: Historicizing Gender and Race*, edited by Ruth Roach Pierson and Nupur Chaudhuri. Bloomington: Indiana University Press, 1997.

Alder, Glenn, and Jonny Steinberg. *From Comrades to Citizens: The South African Civic Movement and the Transition to Democracy*. New York: St. Martin's Press, 2000.

Alexander, Jocelyn, JoAnn McGregor, and Terence Ranger. *Violence and Memory: One Hundred Years in the 'Dark Forests' of Matabeleland Zimbabwe*. Portsmouth, NH: Heinemann, 2000.

Alexander, M. Jacqui, and Chandra Talpade Mohanty, eds. *Feminist Genealogies, Colonial Legacies, Democratic Futures*. New York: Routledge, 1997.

Alexander, Neville. *An Ordinary Country: Issues in the Transition from Apartheid to Democracy in South Africa*. University of Natal Press, 2002.

Alexander, Peter. "Rebellion of the Poor: South Africa's Service Delivery Protests—A Preliminary Analysis." *Review of African Political Economy* 37, no. 123 (2010): 25–40.

Alexander, Peter, Carin Runciman, Trevor Ngwane, Boikanyo Moloto, Kgothatso Mokgele, and Nicole Van Staden. "Frequency and Turmoil: South Africa's Community Protests 2005–2017." *South African Crime Quarterly* 63 (2018): 27–42.

Allatson, Paul. "Stavans's *Latino USA: A Cartoon History* (of a Cosmopolitan Intellectual)." *Chasqui* 35, no. 2 (2006): 21–41.

Allman, Jean. "The Disappearing of Hannah Kudjoe: Nationalism, Feminism, and the Tyrannies of History." *Journal of Women's History* 22, no. 3 (2009): 13–35.

Allman, Jean, Susan Geiger, and Nakanyike Musisi, eds. *Women in African Colonial History*. Bloomington: Indiana University Press, 2002.

Andrew, Rick, Joyce Ozynski, and Harriet Perlman. *Equiano: The Slave Who Fought to Be Free*. Braamfontein: Ravan Press, 1988.

Ashforth, Adam. *The Politics of Official Discourse in Twentieth-Century South Africa*. Oxford: Clarendon Press, 1990.

Ballard, Richard, Adam Habib, and Imraan Valodia, eds. *Voices of Protest: Social Movements in Post-apartheid South Africa.* Pietermaritzburg: University of KwaZulu-Natal Press, 2006.

Baloy, Natalie J.K., Sheeva Sabati, and Ronald David Glass, eds. "Unsettling Research Ethics: A Collaborative Conference Report." UC Center for Collaborative Research for an Equitable California. Santa Cruz: University of California–Santa Cruz, June 30, 2016.

Barnes, Teresa. "'So That a Labourer Could Live with His Family': Overlooked Factors in Social and Economic Strife in Urban Colonial Zimbabwe, 1945–1952." *Journal of Southern African Studies* 21, no. 1 (March 1995): 95–113.

Beinart, William. *Twentieth-Century South Africa.* Cape Town: Oxford University Press, 1994.

Beinart, William, and Collin Bundy. *Hidden Struggles in Rural South Africa: Politics and Popular Movements in the Transkei and Eastern Cape, 1890–1930.* Johannesburg, Ravan Press, 1987.

Benson, Koni. "Collaborative Research in Conversation." In "Body Politics and Censorship." Special issue, *Feminist Africa* 13 (October/November 2009): 107–17.

———. "Crossroads Continues: Histories of Women Mobilizing against Forced Removals and for Housing in Cape Town South Africa, 1975–2005." PhD Dissertation, University of Minnesota, 2009.

———. "Drawing (on) the Past in Histories of the Present: Dialogues and Drawings of South African Women's Organized Resistance to Forced Removals." In *African Cultural Production and the Rhetoric of Humanism*, edited by Lifongo Vetinde and Jean Blaise Samou, 127–49. Lanham, MD: Lexington Books, 2019.

———. "Graphic Novel Histories: Women's Organized Resistance to Slum Clearance in Crossroads South Africa, 1975–2015." In "40th Anniversary of the Writing of African Women's History Part II," eds. Kathleen Sheldon and Judith van Allen. Special issue, *African Studies Review* 59, no. 1 (2016): 199–214.

———. "Life Narratives of Crossroads Women/Récits de vie de femmes de Crossroads." *Aluka: A Digital Library of Resources from Africa.* January 2007, Life Narratives of Crossroads Women. http://www.aluka.org/action/showMetadata?doi=10.5555/AL.SFF.DOCUMENT.ae000011.

———. "A 'Political War of Words and Bullets:' Defining and Defying Sides of Struggle for Housing in Crossroads, South Africa." *Journal of Southern African Studies* 41, no. 2 (2015): 367–87.

Benson, Koni, and Asher Gamedze. "Beyond a Classroom: Experiments in a Post-border Praxis for the Future." In *Critical Methods in Studying World Politics: Creativity and Transformation*, edited by Erzsebet Strausz, Shine Choi, Anna Selmeczi, 121–35. London: Routledge Innovation Series, 2019.

Benson, Koni, Asher Gamedze, and Akosua Koranteng. "African History in Context: Toward a Praxis of Radical Education." In *History's School: Past Struggles and Present Realities*, edited by Aziz Choudry and Salim Vally, 104–17. London: Routledge, 2018.

Benson, Koni, and Faeza Meyer. "Writing My History is Keeping Me Alive: Politics and Practices of Collaborative History Writing." In *A Reflexive Inquiry into Gender Research: Towards a New Paradigm of Knowledge Production and Exploring New Frontiers of Gender Research in Southern Africa*, edited by Pumla Gobodo-Madikizela and Samantha van Schalkwyk, 103–29. Newcastle upon Tyne: Cambridge Scholars Publishing, 2015.

Benson, Koni, and Richa Nagar. "Collaboration as Resistance? Reconsidering the Processes, Products, and Possibilities of Feminist Oral History and Ethnography." *Gender, Place, and Culture: A Journal of Feminist Geography* no. 792 (2007): 581–92.

Bernstein, Hilda. *For Their Triumphs and for Their Tears: Women in Apartheid South Africa*. London: International Defence and Aid Fund for Southern Africa, 1985.

Bickford-Smith, Vivian, Elizabeth Van Heyningen, and Nigel Worden. *Cape Town in the Twentieth Century*. Cape Town: David Philip, 1999.

Biko, Steve. *I Write What I Like*. Chicago: University of Chicago Press, 1978.

Bond, Patrick. *Elite Transitions: From Apartheid to Neoliberalism in South Africa*. London: Pluto, 2005.

———. *Cities of Gold, Townships of Coal: Essays on South Africa's Urban Crisis*. Trenton, NJ: Africa World Press, 2000.

Bond, Patrick, and Angela Tait. "The Failure of Housing Policy in Post-apartheid South Africa." *Urban Forums* 8, no. 1 (1997): 19–41.

Boraine Andrew. "Managing the Urban Crisis, 1986–1989: The Role of the National Management System." *South African Review* 5 (1989): 106–18.

Botes, L., M. Lenka, L. Marais, Z. Matebesi, and K. Sigenu. *The Cauldron of Local Protests: Reasons, Impacts and Lessons Learned*. Bloemfontein, South Africa: University of the Free State, Centre for Development Support, 2007.

Bozzoli, Belinda. *Women of Phokeng; Consciousness, Life Strategy, and Migrancy in South Africa, 1900–1983*. London: James Currey, 1991.

Britton, Hannah, Jennifer Fish, and Sheila Meintjes, eds. *Women's Activism in South Africa: Working Across Divides.* Scottsville, South Africa: University of Kwa-Zulu Natal Press, 2009.

Brown, Chester. *Louis Riel: A Comic-Strip Biography.* Montreal: Drawn and Quarterly, 2006.

Brown, Faizel. "Housing Crisis in Cape Town, Western Cape, 1994–2004." *From the Depths of Poverty: Community Survival in Post-apartheid South Africa.* Center for Civil Society, Research Report 5, no. 1 (2005): 83–107.

Bundy, Colin. *Short-Changed? South Africa Since Apartheid.* Athens: Ohio University Press, 2014.

Buthelezi, Mbongiseni. "Sifuna Umlando Wethu (We Are Looking for Our History): Oral Literature and the Meanings of the Past in Post-apartheid South Africa." PhD thesis, Columbia University, 2012.

Chance, Kerry. "Transitory Citizens: Contentious Housing Practices in Contemporary South Africa." *Social Analysis* 59, no. 3 (2015): 62–84.

Charlton, Sarah. "An Overview of the Housing Policy and Debates, Particularly in Relation to Women." Research report written for the Centre for the Study of Violence and Reconciliation, 2004.

Charney, Craig. "Vigilantes, Clientelism, and the South African State." *Transformations* 16 (1991): 1–28.

Chaskalson, Matthew, Karen Jochelson, and Jeremy Seekings. "Rent Boycotts and the Urban Political Economy." *South African Review* 4 (1987): 53–74.

Coalition against Water Privatisation, the Anti-privatisation Forum, and Public Citizen. "'Nothing for Mahala': The Forced Installation of Prepaid Water Meters in Stretford, Extension 4, Orange Farm, Johannesburg, South Africa." Centre for Civil Society Research Report no. 16, 2004.

Cock, Jacklyn. *Colonels and Cadres: War and Gender in South Africa.* Cape Town: Oxford University Press, 1991.

Cock, Jacklyn, and Laurie Nathan, eds. *War and Society: The Militarisation of South Africa.* Cape Town: David Philip, 1989.

Cole, Josette. *Crossroads: The Politics of Reform and Repression 1976–1986.* Johannesburg: Raven Press, 1987.

———. "When Your Life Is Bitter, You Do Something: Women Squatting in the Western Cape: The Origins of Crossroads and the Role of Women in Its Struggle." MA thesis, University of Cape Town, 1984.

Commission of Enquiry into the Crossroads and Philippi Crisis. *Enquiry Report: Crossroads and Philippi Crisis.* Prepared and presented by Essa Moosa (chairperson), Reverend Mlamli Mfenyana, and Geraldine Coy, November 1998. Cape Town: Commission of Enquiry into the Crossroads and Philippi Crisis.

Cooke, Bill, and Uma Kothari, eds. *Participation: The New Tyranny?* New York: Zed Books, 2001.

Cooper, Frederick. "Conflict and Connection: Rethinking Colonial African History." *American Historical Review* 99, no. 5 (1994): 1516–45.

Cross, Catherine. "Conflict Re-emerges at Crossroads: New Shacklords Battle the City." *HSRC Review* 3, no. 1 (March 2005): 6–7.

Davies van Es, Anna, Leonard Gentle, and Mthetho Xali. "New Social Movements in South Africa: Women's Participation and Women's Leadership." International Labour Research and Information Group working paper, 2005.

Davis, Angela. *The Meaning of Freedom: And Other Difficult Dialogues.* Oakland: AK Press, 2012.

Davis, Mike. *Planet of Slums.* New York: Verso, 2006.

Dawson, Marcelle C., and Luke Sinwell, eds. *Contesting Transformation: Popular Resistance in Twenty-First Century South Africa.* London: Pluto Press, 2012.

Dayan, Hilla. "Regimes of Separation: Israel/Palestine and the Shadow of Apartheid." PhD thesis, New York: New School for Social Research, 2008.

Depelchin, Jacques. *The Silences of African History: Between the Syndromes of Discovery and Abolition.* Dar Es Salaam: Mkuki na Nyota Publishers, 2004.

Desai, Ashwin. *We Are the Poor: Community Struggles in Post-apartheid South Africa.* New York: Monthly Review Press, 2002.

Desai, Ashwin, and Richard Pithouse. "'But We Were Thousands': Dispossession, and Resistance in Mandela Park." Centre for Civil Society Research Report no. 9, November 2003.

du Toit, Pierre, and Jannie Gagiano. "Strongmen on the Cape Flats." *African Insight* 23 (1993): 102–11.

Ellis, George, Delia Hendrie, Alide Kooy, and Johan Maree. *The Squatter Problem in the Western Cape: Some Causes and Remedies.* Johannesburg: South African Institute of Race Relations, 1977.

Enloe, Cynthia. *Maneuvers: The International Politics of Militarizing Women's Lives.* Berkeley: University of California Press, 2000.

Essof, Shereen. "The Feminist Dimension." In *Political Power: State, Party and Popular Power*, edited by Arndt Hopfmann and Leonard Gentle. Proceedings of the Rosa Luxemburg Seminar. Johannesburg: Rosa Luxemburg Foundation, 2007.

Faludi, Susan. *Backlash: The Undeclared War against American Women*. New York: Random House, 1991.

Fast, Hildegarde. "An Overview of African Settlement in the Cape Metropolitan Area to 1990." Urban Problems Research Unit, University of Cape Town, Working Paper no. 53, 1995.

Feminist Alternatives, eds. *My Dream Is to Be Bold: Our Work to End Patriarchy*. Cape Town: Pambazuka Press, 2011.

Fester, Gertrude. "Women's Organizations in the Western Cape: Vehicles for Gender Struggle or Instruments of Subordination?" *Agenda 34* (1997): 45–61.

Field, Sean. *Lost Communities, Living Memories and Remembering Forced Removals in Cape Town*. Cape Town: David Phillip, 2001.

———. "Turning Up the Volume: Dialogues about Memory Create Oral Histories." *South African Historical Journal* 60, no. 2 (2008): 175–94.

Flinn, Andrew. "Working with the Past: Making History of Struggle Part of the Struggle." In In *History's School: Past Struggles and Present Realities*, edited by Aziz Choudry and Salim Vally, 21–42. London: Routledge, 2018.

Flowers, Arthur. *I See the Promised Land: A Life of Martin Luther King, Jr.* Illustrated by Manu Chitrakar. Chennai, India: Tara Books, 2013.

Freund, Bill. *The African City: A History*. Cambridge: Cambridge University Press, 2007.

Frisch, Michael. *A Shared Authority: Essays on the Craft and Meaning of Oral and Public History*. Albany: State University of New York Press, 1990.

Gaitskell, Deborah. "Introduction, Thematic Issue, Women in Southern Africa." *Journal of Southern African Studies* 10, no. 1 (1983): 1–16.

Gasa, Nombonisa, ed. *Women in South African History: They Remove Boulders and Cross Rivers*, Basus'iimbokodo, Bawel'imilambo. Cape Town: HSRC Press, 2007.

Geiger, Susan. "What's So Feminist about Women's Oral History?" *Journal of Women's History* 2, no. 1 (1990): 169–82.

Gengenbach, Heidi. "Truth Telling and the Politics of Women's Life History in Africa: A Reply to Kirk Hoppe." *International Journal of African Historical Studies* 27, no. 3 (1994): 619–27.

Gerhart, Gail. *Black Power in South Africa: The Evolution of an Ideology*. Berkeley: University of California Press, 1978.

Getz, Trevor, and Liz Clarke. *Abina and the Important Men*. New York: Vertigo, 2009.

Ghosh, Vishwajyoti. *This Side, That Side: Restorying Partition: Graphic Narratives from Pakistan, India, Bangladesh*. New Delhi: Yoda Press, 2013.

Giroux, Henry. *Teachers as Intellectuals: Toward a Critical Pedagogy of Learning.* Granby, MA: Bergin & Garvey, 1988.

Gluck, Sherna Berger, and Daphne Patai. *Women's Words: The Feminist Practice of Oral History.* New York: Routledge, 1991.

Goldblatt, Beth, and Sheila Meintjes. "South African Women Demand the Truth." In *What Women Do in Wartime: Gender and Conflict in Africa*, edited by Meredeth Turshen and Clothilde Twagiramariya, 27–61. London: Zed Press, 1998.

Graham, Nick. "Informal Settlement Upgrading in Cape Town: Challenges, Constraints, and Contradictions within Local Government." N2 Gateway Project Workshop, Development Action Group, Cape Town, 2004.

Greenwell, Anne W. "Criminal Strategies of Competing Protagonists in the 'Development' of Crossroads 1990–9." Master's thesis, University of Cape Town, Department of Criminology, 2001.

Gunn, Shirley. *If Trees Could Speak: The Trojan Horse Story.* Cape Town: Human Rights Media Center, 2007.

Hamilton, Carolyn, et al., eds. *Refiguring the Archive.* Cape Town: David Philip, 2002.

Hansson, Desirée, and Dirk Van Zyl Smit. *Towards Justice? Crime and State Control in South Africa.* Cape Town: Oxford University Press, 1990.

Hart, Gillian. *Rethinking the South African Crisis: Nationalism, Populism, Hegemony.* Athens: University of Georgia Press, 2014.

Hassim, Shireen. *Women's Organizations and Democracy in South Africa: Contesting Authority.* Madison: University of Wisconsin Press, 2005.

Haysom, Nicholas. "Vigilantes: A Contemporary Form of Repression." Center for Study of Violence and Reconciliation, University of the Witwatersrand, Seminar no. 4, May 25, 1989.

Hendricks, Ntsebeza, and Helliker. *The Promise of Land: Undoing a Century of Dispossession in South Africa.* Cape Town: Jacana, 2013.

Hirst, Terry, and Davinder Lamba. *The Struggle for Nairobi.* Nairobi: Mazingira Institute, 1994.

Hobsbawm, Eric, and Terence Ranger, eds. *The Invention of Tradition.* Cambridge: Cambridge University Press 1992.

Hodgson, Dorothy L., and Sheryl McCurdy, eds. *"Wicked" Women and the Reconfiguration of Gender in Africa.* Oxford: James Currey, 2001.

hooks, bell. *Teaching to Transgress: Education as the Practice of Freedom.* New York: Routledge, 1994.

Horner, Dudley, ed. *Labour Preference, Influx Control and Squatters: Cape Town Entering the 1980s.* Cape Town: South African Labour and Development Research Unit, SALDRU Working Paper no. 50, July 1983.

Huchzermeyer, Marie. *Cities with 'Slums': From Informal Settlement Eradication to a Right to the City in Africa.* Cape Town: University of Cape Town Press, 2011.

———. "A Legacy of Control? The Capital Subsidy for Housing, and Informal Settlement Intervention in South Africa." *International Journal on Urban and Regional Research* 27, no. 3 (2003): 591–612.

Ibrahim, Abdullahi A. "The Birth of the Interview: The Thin and the Fat of It." In *African Words, African Voices*, edited by Luise White, Stephen Miescher, and David William Cohen, 103–24. Bloomington: Indiana University Press, 2001.

Isaacman, Allen. "Displaced People, Displaced Energy, and Displaced Memories: The Case of Cahora Bassa, 1970–2004." *International Journal of African Historical Studies* 38, no. 2 (2005): 201–38.

Isaacs, Arnold H. "Crossroads: The Rise and Fall of a Squatter Movement." In *Urban Social Movements in the Third World*, edited by Frans J. Schuurman and Ton van Naerssen, 105–24. London: Routledge, 1989.

Japha, Derek, and Marie Hüchzermeyer. "The History of the Development of Townships in Cape Town, 1920–1992." Urbanization Working Paper no. 2. University of Newcastle and University of Cape Town, 1995.

Jordan, June. "Poem for South African Women." In *Passion: New Poems (1977–1980).* Boston: Beacon Press, 1980.

Kaarsholm, Preben. *Cultural Struggle & Development in Southern Africa.* Harare: Baobab, 1991.

Kalabamu, Faustin, Matseliso Mapetla, and Ann Schlyter, eds. *Gender, Generation and Urban Living Conditions in Southern Africa.* Roma, Lesotho: Institute of Southern African Studies, National University of Lesotho, 2005.

Kaplan, Temma. *Crazy for Democracy: Women in Grassroots Movements.* New York: Routledge, 1997.

Kelley, Robin D.G. *Freedom Dreams: The Black Radical Imagination.* Boston: Beacon Press, 2002.

Kerr, Daniel. "We Know What the Problem Is: Using Oral History to Develop a Collaborative Analysis of Homelessness from the Bottom Up." *Oral History Review* 30, no. 1 (2003): 27–47.

Khalane, Len, and Michelle Parlevliet. "UMAC's Militarised Youth Crime Prevention Project: An Evaluation." http://www.umac.org.za, accessed March 13, 2006.

Khan, Firoz. "The N2 Informal Settlement Upgrade Lead Pilot Project." In *Isandla Development Communique 1*, no. 7 (2004).

Khan, Firoz, and Petal Thring, eds. *Housing Policy and Practice in Post-apartheid South Africa*. Sandown, South Africa: Heinemann, 2003.

Khanya College. *GEAR and Housing in South Africa*. Booklet no. 3, February 2001.

Kiewit, Keith, and Kim Weichel. *Inside Crossroads*. Johannesburg: McGraw-Hill, 1980.

Kincead-Weekes, B. "Africans in Cape Town: State Policy and Popular Resistance, 1936–73" PhD dissertation, University of Cape Town, Department of History, 1992.

Kirtley, Susan E., Antero Garcia, and Peter E. Carlson, eds. *With Great Power Comes Great Pedagogy: Teaching, Learning, and Comics*. Jackson: University of Mississippi Press, 2020.

Klein, Naomi. *The Shock Doctrine: The Rise of Disaster Capitalism*. Toronto: Alfred A. Knopf, 2007.

Krog, Antjie, and Nosisi Mpolweni. "Archived Voices: Refiguring Three Women's Testimonies Delivered to the Truth and Reconciliation Commission." *Tulsa Studies in Women's Literature* 28, no. 2 (2009): 357–74.

Kwinjeh, Grace. "Feminist Reflections on Gender Violence, Political Power and Women's Emancipation: From Rhodesia to Present Day Zimbabwe." *Pambazuka News*, December 4, 2007, https://www.pambazuka.org/gender-minorities/feminist-reflections-gender-violence-political-power-and-women's-emancipation.

Lalu, Premesh. "The Virtual Stampede for Africa: Digitisation, Postcoloniality and Archives of the Liberation Struggles in Southern Africa." *Innovation* 34 (June 2007): 28–44.

Lawyers Committee for Human Rights. *Crisis in Crossroads: A Report on Human Rights in South Africa*. New York: Lawyers Committee for Human Rights, 1987.

Lee, Rebekah. "Reconstructing 'Home' in Apartheid Cape Town: African Women and the Process of Settlement." *Journal of Southern African Studies* 31, no. 3 (2005): 611–30.

Legassick, Martin. "Ten Years of Freedom: The Case of Mandela Park, Khayelitsha." University of Western Cape, Contemporary History Seminar Paper, August 10, 2004.

———. "Direct Action: Housing Battles in Post-apartheid South Africa." *Debate: Voices from the South Africa Left* 11 (March 2005): 17–23.

Levenson, Zachary. "The Road to TRAs is Paved with Good Intentions: Dispossession through Delivery in Post-apartheid Cape Town." *International Journal of Urban and Regional Research* 27, no. 3 (2017): 591–612.

Lohnert, Oldfield, and Parnell. "Post-apartheid Social Polarisations: The Creation of Sub-urban Identities in Cape Town." *South African Geographical Journal* 80, no. 2 (1998): 86–92.

MacPhee, Josh, Shaun Slifer, and Bec Young, eds. *Firebrands: Portraits from the Americas.* Justseeds Artists' Cooperative. Portland: Microcosm Publishing, 2010.

Mager, Anne Kelk. *Gender and the Making of a South African Bantustan: A Social History of the Ciskei, 1945–1959.* New York: Heinemann, 1999.

Magubane, Bernard "The Political Economy of the South African Revolution." *African Journal of Political Economy* 1, no. 1 (1986): 1–28.

Makhulu, Anne-Marie. *Making Freedom: Apartheid, Squatter Politics, and the Struggle for Home.* Durham, NC: Duke University Press, 2015.

Mamdani, Mahmood. *Citizen and Subject: Contemporary Africa and the Legacy of Late Colonialism.* Princeton NJ: Princeton University Press, 1996.

———. "Reconciliation Without Justice." *Southern Review* 10 no. 6 (March 1997): 22–25.

Manicom, Lindzi. "Ruling Relations: Rethinking State and Gender in South African History." *The Journal of African History* 33, no. 3 (1992): 441–65.

Maree, Johann, and Judith Cornell. "Sample Survey of Squatters in Crossroads: December 1977." Cape Town: SALDRU Working Paper no. 17, 1978.

Marx, Anthony W. *Lessons of Struggle: South African Internal Opposition, 1960–1990.* New York: Oxford University Press, 1992.

McDonald and Pape, *Cost Recovery and the Crisis of Service Delivery in South Africa.* Cape Town: Human Sciences Research Council Publishers, 2002.

McFadden, Patricia. Political Power: The Challenges of Sexuality, Patriarchy and Globalization in Africa. Port Louis, Mauritius: Ledikasyon pu travayer, 2001.

McKinley, Dale. "Riding the Transitional Rollercoaster: The Shifting Relationship between Civil Society and the Constitution in Post-apartheid South Africa." Johannesburg: South African History Archive, 2015.

McKinley, Dale, and P. Naidoo, eds. "Mobilizing for Change, The Rise of the New Social Movements in South Africa." Special issue, *Development Update* 5, no. 2 (November 2004): 9–22.

McKinley, Dale, and Ahmed Veriava. *Arresting Dissent: State Repression and Post-apartheid Social Movements.* Johannesburg: Centre for the Study of Violence and Reconciliation, 2005.

Mda, Zakes. *Four Plays: Compiled and Introduced by Zakes Mda.* Florida Hills, South Africa: Vivlia Publications, 1996.

Meer, Shamim. *Women Speak! Reflections on Our Struggles, 1982–1992.* Johannesburg: Kwela Books, 1998.

Meintjes, Sheila. "Gender, Nationalism and Transformation: Difference and Commonality in South Africa's Past and Present." In *Women, Ethnicity and Nationalism: The Politics of Transition,* edited by Rick Wilford and Robert L. Miller, 60–82. London: Routledge, 1998.

Minkley, Gary, and Nicky Rousseau. "'This Narrow Language': People's History and the University: Reflections from the University of the Western Cape." *South African Historical Journal* 34 (1996): 175–95.

Miraftab, Faranak. "Feminist Praxis, Citizenship and Informal Politics: Reflections on South Africa's Anti-eviction Campaign." *International Feminist Journal of Politics* 8, no. 2 (June 2006): 194–218.

———. "The Perils of Participatory Discourse: Housing Policy in Post-apartheid South Africa." *Journal of Planning Education and Research* 22 (2003): 226–39.

Mnguni (Hosea Jaffe). *Three Hundred Years.* Unity Movement Series, published by African People's Democratic Union of Southern Africa, APDUSA, 1952.

Mohanty, Chandra. *Feminism without Borders: Decolonizing Theory, Practicing Solidarity.* Durham, NC: Duke University Press, 2003.

Moser, Caroline, and Fiona Clark, eds. *Victims, Perpetrators or Actors? Gender, Armed Conflict and Political Violence.* London: Zed Books, 2001.

Moss, Glenn, and Ingrid Obery, eds. *South African Review* 4. Johannesburg: Ravan Press, 1987.

Murray, Martin. *South Africa: Time of Agony, Time of Destiny: The Upsurge of Popular Protest.* London: Verso, 1987.

———. *The Revolution Deferred: The Painful Birth of Post-apartheid South Africa.* London: Verso, 1994.

Muthien, Yvonne. *State and Resistance in South Africa, 1939–65.* Brookfield: Avebury, 1994.

Nagar, Richa. *Muddying the Waters: Coauthoring Feminisms across Scholarship and Activism.* Urbana: Illinois University Press, 2014.

Namhila, Ellen Ndeshi. "Transforming the Traumatic Life Experiences of Women in Post-apartheid Namibian Historical Narratives." In *Re-viewing Resistance in Namibian History,* edited by Jeremy Silvester, 22–37. Windhoek, UNAM Press, 2015.

National Union of South African Students. *Nyanga Bush: The Story of the Squatters*. Students for Social Democracy and NUSAS. University of Cape Town, Student Representative Committee Press, 1981.

———. *We Will Not Move: The Struggle for Crossroads*. Cape Town: NUSAS, 1978.

Neuwirth, Robert. *Shadow Cities: A Billion Squatters, a New Urban World*. New York: Routledge, 2006.

Ngwane, Zolani. "'Christmas Time' and the Struggles for the Household in the Countryside: Rethinking the Cultural Geography of Migrant Labour in South Africa." *Journal of Southern African Studies* 29, no. 3 (September 2003): 681–99.

Nieftagodien, Noor. *The Soweto Uprising*. Athens: Ohio University Press, 2015.

Norval, Aletta J. *Deconstructing Apartheid Discourse*. London: Verso, 1996.

Nutall, Sarah, and Coetzee, Carli, eds. *Negotiating the Past: The Making of Memory in South Africa*. Cape Town: Oxford University Press, 1998.

Oldfield, Sophie, and Saskia Greyling. "Waiting for the State: A Politics of Housing in South Africa." *Environment and Planning* 47, no. 5 (2015): 1100–12.

Pandey, Gyanendra. *Memory, History, and the Question of Violence*. Calcutta: Centre for Studies in Social Sciences, 1999.

Parnell, Susan. "State Intervention in Housing Provision in the 1980s." In *The Apartheid City and Beyond*, edited by David M. Smith, 53–64. London: Routledge, 1992.

Patel, Leila. "South African Women's Struggles in the 1980s." *Agenda* 2 (1988): 28–35.

Perkins, Kathy. *Black South African Women: An Anthology of Plays*. London, Routledge, 1999.

Perks, Robert, and Alistair Thomson. *The Oral History Reader*. New York: Routledge, 2015.

Peterson, Derek, Kodzo Gavua, and Ciraj Rassool, eds. *The Politics of Heritage in Africa: Economies, Histories and Infrastructures*. Cambridge University Press, 2015.

Phillips, Mark. "Divide and Repress: Vigilantes and State Objectives in Crossroads." In *States of Terror*, 15–35. Catholic Institute for International Relations, 1989.

Pithouse, Richard. "'Our Struggle Is Thought, on the Ground, Running,' The University of Abahlali BaseMjondolo." University of KwaZulu Natal: Center for Civil Society Research Report no. 40, 2006.

Plaaitje, Sol. *Native Life in South Africa*. London: P.S. King and Son, 1914.

Platzky, Laurine, and Cherryl Walker. *The Surplus People: Forced Removals in South Africa*. Johannesburg: Ravan, 1985.

Pohlandt-McCormick, Helena. *"I Saw a Nightmare . . .": Doing Violence to Memory, The Soweto Uprising, June 16, 1976*. New York: Columbia University Press, 2005.

Portelli, Alessandro. "The Peculiarities of Oral History." *History Workshop* no. 12 (Autumn 1981): 96–107.

Posel, Deborah. *The Making of Apartheid, 1948–1961: Conflict and Compromise*. New York: Clarendon Press, 1991.

Posel, Deborah, and Graeme Simpson, eds. *Commissioning the Past: Understanding South Africa's Truth and Reconciliation Commission*. Johannesburg: Witwatersrand University Press, 2003.

Ramphele, Mamphela. *A Bed Called Home: Life in the Migrant Labour Hostels*. Cape Town: David Phillip, 1993.

———. *Steering by the Stars: Being Young in South Africa*. South Africa: Tafelberg Publishers, 2002.

Ramutsindela, Maano. "The Enduring Spatial Legacy of the Natives Land Act." *Social Dynamics: A Journal of African Studies* 39, no. 2 (2013): 290–97.

———. "'Second Time Around': Squatter Removals in a Democratic South Africa." *GeoJournal* 57 (2002): 53–60.

Rantete, Johannes. *The Third Day of September: An Eye-witness Account of the Sebokeng Rebellion of 1984*. Johannesburg: Ravan Press, 1984.

Reddy, Thiven. *South Africa: Settler Colonialism and the Failures of Liberal Democracy*. Johannesburg: Witwatersrand University Press, 2016.

Robins, Steven. "Bodies out of Place: Crossroads and the Landscapes of Exclusion." In *Blank: Architecture, Apartheid and After*, edited by Hilton Judin and Ivan Vladislavic. Cape Town: David Philips, 1999.

Ross, Fiona. *Bearing Witness: Women and the Truth and Reconciliation Commission in South Africa*. London: Pluto Press, 2003.

Rouverol, Alicia. "Collaborative Oral History in a Correctional Setting: Promise and Pitfalls." *Oral History Review* 30 (2003): 61–87.

Runciman, Carin. "The Decline of the Anti-privatisation Forum in the Midst of South Africa's 'Rebellion of the Poor.'" *Current Sociology* 63, no. 7 (2014): 961–79.

Sacco, Joe. *Palestine*. Seattle: Fantagraphics Books, 2001.

Salo, Elaine. "Multiple Targets, Mixing Strategies: Complicating Feminist Analysis of Contemporary South African Women's Movements." *Feminist Africa* 4 (2005): 64–71.

Sangtin Writers and Richa Nagar. *Playing with Fire: Feminist Thought and Activism through Seven Lives in India.* Minneapolis: University of Minnesota Press, 2006.

Saul, John. *A Flawed Freedom: Rethinking Southern African Liberation.* Pluto Press, 2014.

Saunders, Christopher. "The Creation of Ndabeni: Urban Segregation and African Resistance in Cape Town." *Studies in the History of Cape Town* 1 (1979): 165–87.

———. "From Ndabeni to Langa, 1919–1935." *Studies in the History of Cape Town* 1 (1979): 19–24.

Scott, James. *Seeing like a State: How Certain Schemes to Improve the Human Condition Have Failed.* New Haven, CT: Yale University Press, 1998.

Scott, Joan. "The Evidence of Experience." *Critical Inquiry* 17, no. 4 (Summer 1991): 773–97.

Scully, Pamela, and Clifton Crais. *Sara Baartman and the Hottentot Venus: A Ghost Story and a Biography.* Princeton, NJ: Princeton University Press, 2008.

Seekings, Jeremy. *The UDF: A History of the United Democratic Front in South Africa, 1983–1991.* Cape Town: David Philip, 2000.

Seleoane, Mandla. "Nyanga East Men's Hostel: The Condition of Migrant Workers." SALDRU Working Paper no. 62, University of Cape Town, May 1985.

Shopes, Linda. "Beyond Trivia and Nostalgia: Collaborating in the Construction of a Local History." *International Journal of Oral History* 5 (1984): 151–58.

Shubane, Khehla. "Black Local Authorities: A Contraption of Control." In *Apartheid City in Transition*, edited by Mark Swilling, Richard Humphries, and Shubane Khehla, 64–77. Cape Town: Oxford University Press, 1991.

Silk, Andrew. *A Shanty Town in South Africa: The Story of Modderdam.* Johannesburg: Ravan Press, 1985.

Sisk, Timothy. *Democratization in South Africa: The Elusive Social Contract.* Princeton, NJ: Princeton University Press, 1995.

Sithole, Jabulani, and Sifiso Ndlovu. "The Revival of the Labour Movement, 1970–1980." In *The Road to Democracy in South Africa, Vol. 2*, 187–241. Pretoria: UNISA, 2014.

Soursar, Mosireen "858: No Archive Is Innocent: On the Attempt of Archiving Revolt" (nd), https://www.mosireen.com/-no-archive-is-innocent, accessed February 17, 2020.

South African Government. *Enquiry Report: Crossroads and Philippi Crisis.* Prepared and presented by Essa Moosa (chairperson), Reverend Mlamli Mfenyana, and Geraldine Coy. November 1998.

Srigley, K., S. Zembrzychi, and F. Iacovetta, eds. *Beyond Women's Words: Feminisms and the Practices of Oral History in the Twenty-First Century.* London: Routledge, 2018.

Stoler, Ann Laura. "Colonial Archives and the Arts of Governance." *Archival Science* 2 (2002): 87–109.

Tabata, I.B. *Apartheid: Cosmetics Exposed.* London: Prometheus Publications for Unity Movement of South Africa, 1986.

Terreblanche, Sampie. *A History of Inequality in South Africa 1652–2002.* Pietermaritzburg: University of Natal Press, 2002.

Tissington, Kate, Naadira Munshi, Gladys Mirugi-Mukundi, and Ebenezer Durojaye. *"Jumping the Queue," Waiting Lists and Other Myths: Perceptions and Practice around Housing Demand and Allocation in South Africa.* Community Law Centre, University of the Western Cape/Socio-economic Rights Institute of South Africa, 2013.

Tomlinson, Mary R. "From 'Quantity' to 'Quality': Restructuring South Africa's Housing Policy Ten Years After." *International Development Planning Review* 28, no. 1 (2006): 85–104.

Trantraal, André, Charmaine Trantraal, and Nathan Trantraal. *Coloureds. Underdog Comics* no. 1. Bishop Lavis, South Africa: Jincom, 2010.

Trouillot, Michel-Rolph. Silencing the Past: Power and the Production of History. Boston: Beacon Press, 1995.

Truth and Reconciliation Commission of South Africa. *Truth and Reconciliation Commission Report,* vols. 1–5. Cape Town: Truth and Reconciliation Commission, 1998.

van Donk, Mirjan, and Edgar Pieterse. "Reflections of the Design of the Post-apartheid System of (Urban) Local Government." In *Democracy and Delivery: Urban Policy in South Africa,* edited by Udesh Pillay, Richard Tomlinson, and Jacques du Toit. Cape Town, HSRC Press, 2006.

van Heusden, Peter, and Rebecca Pointer. "Subjectivity, Politics and Neoliberalism in Post-apartheid Cape Town." *Journal of Asian and African Studies* 41, no. 1 (2006): 95–121.

Wacks, Jonathan. *Crossroads/South Africa: The Struggle Continues.* Documentary film, Schomburg Collection, New York Public Library, 1980.

Walker, Cherryl. *Women and Resistance in South Africa.* Cape Town: David Philip, 1982.

Watson, Vanessa. "Conflicting Rationalities: Implications for Planning Theory and Ethics." *Planning Theory and Practice* 4, no. 5 (2003): 395–407.

Wegerif, Marc, Bev Russel, and Irma Grundling. *Still Searching for Security: The Reality of Farm Dweller Evictions in South Africa*. Polokwane: Nkuzi Development Association / Johannesburg: Social Surveys, 2005.

Weichel, K, L. Smith, and M. Putterill. "Nyanga and Crossroads: Some Aspects of Social and Economic Activity." University of Cape Town: Urban Problems Research Unit, February 1978.

Wells, Julia C. "Why Women Rebel: A Comparative Study of South African Women's Resistance in Bloemfontein (1913) and Johannesburg (1958)." *Journal of Southern African Studies* 10, no. 1 (1983): 55–70.

Western, John. *Outcast Cape Town*. Berkeley: University of California Press, 1996.

Williams, John. "Community Participation and Democratic Practice in Post-apartheid South Africa: Rhetoric vs. Reality." *Policy Studies* 27, no. 3 (September 2006): 197–217.

Wilson, Lindy. *Crossroads: A Film by Lindy Wilson*. Narrated by Janet Suzman. Edited by Terry Pantling. September 1978.

Witz, Leslie, Gary Minkley, and Ciraj Rassool, eds. *Unsettled History: Making South African Pasts*. Ann Arbor: University of Michigan Press, 2017.

Worden, Nigel. *The Making of Modern South Africa: Conquest, Segregation and Apartheid*. Oxford: Blackwell, 1994.

Xulu-Gama, Nomkhosi. *Hostels in South Africa: Spaces of Perplexity*. Pietermaritzburg: KwaZulu-Natal Press, 2017.

Zinn, Howard. *You Can't Be Neutral on a Moving Train: A Personal History of Our Times*. Boston: Beacon Press, 1994.

About the Authors and Illustrators

Koni Benson is a historian, organizer, and educator. She is a lecturer in the Department of History at the University of the Western Cape, in Cape Town South Africa. Since 2006 she has been coproducing life histories of self-organization and unfolding political struggles of collective resistance in struggles for land and public services such as housing, water, and education in South Africa. She is committed to creative approaches to history that link art, activism, and African history, and draws on critical approaches to people's history projects, popular education, and feminist collaborative research praxis, in her work with archives and with various student, activist, and cultural collectives in southern Africa.

André Trantraal is a writer, illustrator, and translator from Bishop Lavis, Cape Town. He is the writer of the comic books *Coloureds* and *Stormkaap*. His work has been exhibited in Amsterdam, Hamburg, and Cape Town and his political cartoons have appeared in a range of South African newspapers.

Nathan Trantraal is a poet, cartoonist, translator, playwright, screenwriter, short story author, and columnist. He was awarded the Ingrid Jonker Prize for poetry, and his work has been exhibited in Cape Town, Munich, and Amsterdam. His comics have been published in various South African newspapers. He is currently a lecturer at Rhodes University at the School of Languages, where he specializes in Kaapse Afrikaans and the graphic novel.

Ashley E. Marais is a comic book artist, designer, and painter. With the Trantraal Brothers, he was coauthor and illustrator on the graphic novel *Stormkaap* and the comic book *Coloureds*, both of which are in the Cape Afrikaans language. Also with the Trantraal Brothers, he is joint illustrator of

Safety, Justice & People's Power, a book about the Khayelitsha Commission, written by Richard Conyngham.

Robin D.G. Kelley is an American historian and distinguished author, activist, and teacher who is currently the Gary B. Nash Professor of American History at UCLA. He has held posts at Oxford, NYU, and Columbia. His research focuses of social movements in the U.S., the African Diaspora, and Africa; black intellectuals; music; visual culture; contemporary urban studies; historiography and historical theory; poverty studies and ethnography; colonialism/ imperialism; organized labor; constructions of race; Surrealism, Marxism, nationalism, among other things. Kelley's work includes seven books as well as over one hundred magazine articles. He is the author of *Freedom Dreams: The Black Radical Imagination*; *Hammer and Hoe: Alabama Communists During the Great Depression*; *Race Rebels: Culture, Politics, and the Black Working Class*; *Imagining Home: Class, Culture, and Nationalism in the African Diaspora*; *Into the Fire: African Americans Since 1970*; *Yo' Mama's DisFunktional!: Fighting the Culture Wars in Urban America*; *Three Strikes: The Fighting Spirit of Labor's Last Century*; and *Thelonious Monk: The Life and Times of an American Original*.

PM Press is an independent, radical publisher of books and media to educate, entertain, and inspire. Founded in 2007 by a small group of people with decades of publishing, media, and organizing experience, PM Press amplifies the voices of radical authors, artists, and activists. Our aim is to deliver bold political ideas and vital stories to all walks of life and arm the dreamers to demand the impossible. We have sold millions of copies of our books, most often one at a time, face to face. We're old enough to know what we're doing and young enough to know what's at stake. Join us to create a better world.

PM Press
PO Box 23912
Oakland CA 94623
510-658-3906
www.pmpress.org

PM Press in Europe
europe@pmpress.org
www.pmpress.org.uk

FRIENDS OF PM

These are indisputably momentous times—the financial system is melting down globally and the Empire is stumbling. Now more than ever there is a vital need for radical ideas.

In the many years since its founding—and on a mere shoestring—PM Press has risen to the formidable challenge of publishing and distributing knowledge and entertainment for the struggles ahead. With hundreds of releases to date, we have published an impressive and stimulating array of literature, art, music, politics, and culture. Using every available medium, we've succeeded in connecting those hungry for ideas and information to those putting them into practice.

Friends of PM allows you to directly help impact, amplify, and revitalize the discourse and actions of radical writers, filmmakers, and artists. It provides us with a stable foundation from which we can build upon our early successes and provides a much-needed subsidy for the materials that can't necessarily pay their own way. You can help make that happen—and receive every new title automatically delivered to your door once a month—by joining as a Friend of PM Press. And, we'll throw in a free T-shirt when you sign up.

Here are your options:
- $30 a month: Get all books and pamphlets plus 50% discount on all webstore purchases
- $40 a month: Get all PM Press releases (including CDs and DVDs) plus 50% discount on all webstore purchases
- $100 a month: Superstar—Everything plus PM merchandise, free downloads, and 50% discount on all webstore purchases

For those who can't afford $30 or more a month, we have Sustainer Rates at $15, $10, and $5. Sustainers get a free PM Press T-shirt and a 50% discount on all purchases from our website.

Your Visa or Mastercard will be billed once a month, until you tell us to stop. Or until our efforts succeed in bringing the revolution around. Or the financial meltdown of Capital makes plastic redundant. Whichever comes first.

SIGNAL
A Journal of International
Political Graphics & Culture
Edited by Josh MacPhee and Alec Dunn
$14.95

Signal is an ongoing book series dedicated to documenting and sharing compelling graphics, art projects, and cultural movements of international resistance and liberation struggles. Artists and cultural workers have been at the center of upheavals and revolts the world over, from the painters and poets in the Paris Commune to the poster-makers and street-theatre performers of the Occupy movement. *Signal* brings these artists and their work to a new audience, digging deep through our common history to unearth their images and stories.

In the US there is a tendency to focus only on the artworks produced within our shores or from English-speaking producers. *Signal* reaches beyond those bounds, bringing material produced the world over, translated from dozens of languages and collected from both the present and decades past. Although a full-color printed publication, *Signal* is not limited to the graphic arts. Within its pages you will find political posters and fine arts, comics and murals, street art, site-specific works, zines, art collectives, documentation of performances, and articles on the often-overlooked but essential roles all of these have played in struggles around the world.

ISBN: 978-1-60486-091-7

ISBN: 978-1-60486-298-0

ISBN: 978-1-60486-362-8

ISBN: 978-1-62963-106-6

ISBN: 978-1-62963-156-1

ISBN: 978-1-62963-387-9

COUNTERPOINTS
A San Francisco Bay Area Atlas of Displacement & Resistance
Anti-Eviction Mapping Project
Foreword by Ananya Roy & Chris Carlsson
ISBN: 978-1-62963-828-7 • $34.95

Counterpoints: A San Francisco Bay Area Atlas of Displacement and Resistance brings together cartography, essays, illustrations, poetry, and more in order to depict gentrification and resistance struggles from across the San Francisco Bay Area and act as a roadmap to counter-hegemonic knowledge making and activism. Compiled by the Anti-Eviction Mapping Project, each chapter reflects different frameworks for understanding the Bay Area's ongoing urban upheaval, including: evictions and root shock, indigenous geographies, health and environmental racism, state violence, transportation and infrastructure, migration and relocation, and speculative futures. By weaving these themes together, *Counterpoints* expands normative urban-studies framings of gentrification to consider more complex, regional, historically grounded, and entangled horizons for understanding the present. Understanding the tech boom and its effects means looking beyond San Francisco's borders to consider the region as a socially, economically, and politically interconnected whole and reckoning with the area's deep history of displacement, going back to its first moments of settler colonialism. *Counterpoints* combines work from within the project with contributions from community partners, from longtime community members who have been fighting multiple waves of racial dispossession to elementary school youth envisioning decolonial futures. In this way, *Counterpoints* is a collaborative, co-created atlas aimed at expanding knowledge on displacement and resistance in the Bay Area with, rather than for or about, those most impacted.

MAROON COMIX
Origins and Destinies
Edited by Quincy Saul
Illustrated by Seth Tobocman, Mac McGill, and Songe Riddle
ISBN: 978-1-62963-571-2 • $15.95

Escaping slavery in the Americas, maroons made miracles in the mountains, summoned new societies in the swamps, and forged new freedoms in the forests. They didn't just escape and steal from plantations—they also planted and harvested polycultures. They not only fought slavery but proved its opposite, and for generations they defended it with blood and brilliance.

Maroon Comix is a fire on the mountain where maroon words and images meet to tell stories together. Stories of escape and homecoming, exile and belonging. Stories that converge on the summits of the human spirit, where the most dreadful degradation is overcome by the most daring dignity. Stories of the damned who consecrate their own salvation.

With selections and citations from the writings of Russell Maroon Shoatz, Herbert Aptheker, C.L.R. James, and many more, accompanied by comics and illustrations from Songe Riddle, Mac McGill, Seth Tobocman, and others, *Maroon Comix* is an invitation to never go back, to join hands and hearts across space and time with the maroons and the mountains that await their return.

THE YOUNG C.L.R. JAMES
A Graphic Novelette
Illustrated by Milton Knight
Edited by Paul Buhle and Lawrence Ware
ISBN: 9781629635149 • $6.95

This unique comic by Milton Knight illuminates the early years of C.L.R. James (1901–1989), known in much later years as the "last great Pan-Africanist." The son of a provincial school administrator in British-governed Trinidad, James disappointed his family by embracing the culture and passions of the colonial underclass, Carnival and cricket. He joined the literary avant-garde of the island before leaving for Britain. In the UK, James swiftly became a beloved cricket journalist, playwright for his close friend Paul Robeson, and a pathbreaking scholar of black history with *The Black Jacobins* (1938), the first history of the Haitian revolt.

The artistic skills of Milton Knight, at once acute and provocative, bring out James's unique personality, how it arose, and how he became a world figure.

THE REAL COST OF PRISONS COMIX
Edited by Lois Ahrens
Written by Ellen Miller-Mack, Craig Gilmore, Lois Ahrens, Susan Willmarth, and Kevin Pyle
Illustrated by Kevin Pyle, Sabrina Jones, and Susan Willmarth
Introduction by Craig Gilmore and Ruth Wilson Gilmore
ISBN: 978-1-60486-034-4 • $14.95

Winner of the 2008 PASS Award (Prevention for a Safer Society) from the National Council on Crime and Delinquency

One out of every hundred adults in the US is in prison. This book provides a crash course in what drives mass incarceration, the human and community costs, and how to stop the numbers from going even higher. Collected in this volume are the three comic books published by the Real Cost of Prisons Project. The stories and statistical information in each comic book are thoroughly researched and documented.

Over 125,000 copies of the comic books have been printed and more than 100,000 have been sent to people who are incarcerated, to their families, and to organizers and activists throughout the country. The book includes a chapter with descriptions of how the comix have been put to use in the work of organizers and activists in prison and in the "free world" by ESL teachers, high school teachers, college professors, students, and health care providers throughout the country. The demand for the comix is constant and the ways in which they are being used are inspiring.